UNBELIEVABLE!

FAITH, REASON, AND THE SEARCH FOR TRUTH

Pisgah Press was established in 2011 to publish and promote works of quality offering original ideas and insight into the human condition and the world around us.

Copyright © 2011 Pisgah Press

Printed in the United States of America

Published by Pisgah Press, LLC
PO Box 1427, Candler, NC 28715
www.pisgahpress.com

Book & cover design: A. D. Reed, MyOwnEditor.com
Cover photo by Joseph R. Haun

All rights reserved. No part of this publication may be reproduced, stored in a retrieval system, or transmitted, in any form or by any means, electronic, mechanical, photocopying, recording, or otherwise, without the prior written permission of Pisgah Press, except in the case of quotations in critical articles or reviews.

Library of Congress Cataloging-in-Publication Data
Haun, Joseph R.
Unbelievable: Faith, Reason, and the Search for Truth/Joe Haun

Library of Congress Control Number: 2011939578

Includes bibliographical references and index
ISBN-10: 0615517374
ISBN-13: 978-0615517377
Philosophy / Ethics & Moral philosophy

First Edition
Oct. 2011
Second Printing
February 2012

Acknowledgments

My family has been a constant source of inspiration, with all the memories of their lives, and their patience and encouragement in my pursuit of our combined aspirations. Though there may be elements of disjunction among our basic beliefs, hopefully, the thrust of this book is an attempt to synthesize their contribution to the betterment of humankind.

To Andrew Reed, who shepherded me through the trenches of writing *non*scientific material and helped me explain and organize my memories, I bestow my utmost appreciation. His willingness to attach his name to the effort underlies his endorsement. Further, I wish to acknowledge all the humanitarian things he has done and about which he also has written. Thanks to Sue Stone and the late Harold Johnson for their help in adapting my *Reality Moves On* to music, and to Sharon Fennell for allowing me to include her kind words and memories of Ruth.

Many thanks to my staunch friend and organic chemistry authority, Nelson Sartoris, for the parts documenting scientific proof for the possibility that all creation could have been "by chance alone," and for his analysis of Kevin Phillips's *American Theocracy*. Profound appreciation to Paul Kurtz for all the quotations I have utilized for expressing my philosophy of Humanism. To E. O. Wilson I owe my earliest confirmation of thoughts on sociobiology and my understanding of biological connections with the origin of religion and its ultimate relations to evolution. Thanks to writers and thinkers Jimmy Carter, Richard Dawkins, Daniel Dennett, Sam Harris, Christopher Hitchens, Kevin Phillips, Steven Pinker, and Jeff Sharlet for the many worthwhile impressions, not specifically cited, that have helped shape my own insights and remain clear in my mind. And thanks to many friends who read and commented on the book before it went to print: my five sons and my grandson Ben Haun, Bob Andersen, Cecil Bothwell, Jere Brittain, Carol Emmet, Fred Flaxman, Monroe Gilmour, Nelda Holder, Michael Hopping, Jeff Hutchins, Seymour Meyerson, and Peg Rhodes.

Foreword

Now that you've picked up this book, you're in for a great ride. Belly-landing a Navy training plane, developing the Haun scale to measure plant growth, actively pursuing campaign finance reform, and thinking through life's most important questions, you will be part of Joe Haun's fascinating, inspiring, important life journey.

Several years ago, as a community organizer for WNC Citizens Ending Institutional Bigotry (WNCCEIB), I invited Joe over to talk justice issues and to walk the loop trail my family had built on the mountain above our home. The trail is up and down and steep, even requiring ropes in places. About halfway through the trek, I asked Joe how old he was. Eighty-four, he said. I was floored! What in the world was I doing putting him through that ordeal?

I needn't have worried. Even today at almost 90, Joe looks 75 and is just as energetic and engaged as he has been his entire life.

Our talk that day opened me to Joe's intellectual curiosity, rigor, and wisdom. If the term "Renaissance man" ever applied to anyone, it applies to Joe Haun: in this book, he lets everyone in on his creative and stimulating mind.

Joe is an accomplished scientist, yet he is a scientist with a uniquely uplifting approach to those aspects of human behavior that aren't subject to the rigors of the scientific method: matters of the spirit and the nature of what we commonly call the "soul." The narrative of his life's journey allows us to understand, as the title suggests, *his* faith, reason, and search for truth. What he finds *Unbelievable*—what is at the heart of that search—is how fundamentalist religions create a sacred narrative that, as he puts it, "ignores scientific evidence they can't refute in favor of convictions they cannot substantiate." His consternation cannot but raise serious concerns about what such fundamentalism is doing to our society, our environment, and our democracy.

And those institutions matter to Joe; he wants us to learn about his life, not just because it's a fascinating in and of itself, but in the hope that his journey will help inspire readers to act to preserve and invigorate our local, national, and world community. His chapter titled "Do Something Worthwhile" recommends many organizations doing effective work and highlights Planned Parenthood,

Habitat for Humanity, the Carter Center, and the American Friends Service Committee. Like everything in his life, Joe doesn't simply talk about them; he has worked with and helped finance these and many other organizations.

In my own work supporting victims of hate activity, shielding from demonstrators patients entering a woman's clinic, nudging institutions on diversity issues, and standing with those affected by discrimination, I have observed Joe's active involvement in the world. Most recently, on numerous occasions he accompanied to court a mother whose family had had a cross burned in their yard. His and WNCCEIB's presence gave the mother the courage to see the convictions through and to speak at the sentencing of those who had carried out the act.

What underpins Joe's commitment to justice and service is his humanity. His devotion to his family is beautiful, and we readers can delight in their adventures and travel, from the Shenandoah Valley to Kentucky, Connecticut, Maryland, Georgia, Delaware, South Carolina, North Carolina, and around the world. All of them— his beloved first wife, Ruth, who died in 1978; the five sons they raised together; and Helen, his wonderful wife of the past thirty years—experienced the richness of a life that celebrates both the mind and the hands.

Toward the end of the book we see Joe's love of nature and awe of life's intricacies in a photo of him standing at the base of a tall, tall California redwood tree. He notes that one day his true satisfaction will come in having his ashes sprinkled there where his own atoms can, over time, become part of something so grand and majestic. Truth be told, they already are.

Monroe Gilmour, Executive Director
WNC Citizens Ending Institutional Bigotry
Asheville, NC   September 2011

TABLE OF CONTENTS

Foreword v
Introduction ix
A Note on Words and their Meanings xi

FAITH

Chapter 1   The Shenandoah Valley 3
    New England and Pennsylvania 7
    Nashville 10
Chapter 2   The Larger World 17
    The Cumberland Homesteads 21
Chapter 3   Education, Formal and Informal 25
    Berea, Kentucky 27
Chapter 4   World War II 33
    Ground School 34
    Flying 36
Chapter 5   Graduate School 41
    Political Awakening 42
    Plant Science 44
    DuPont 46
    The Turning Point 48

REASON

Chapter 6   Baltimore Interlude 51
    New Crops for the Country 54
    Pharmaceutical 55
    Oilseeds 56
    Fiber Crops for Paper 57
Chapter 7   Savannah-Richmond Hill Interlude 63
    New Crop Triumphs 64
    Environmental Factors in Plant Growth 65
    Family 67
    A Sudden Loss: the author's letter to friends 73
    Memories from Sharon Fennell 76
Chapter 8   A New Start 87
    Behind the Iron Curtain 90
    The "Leisure" of Retirement 96

Stone Work 97
"Soul" Work 102
Community Work – Ethics in Politics 105

THE SEARCH FOR TRUTH

Chapter 9   Imagination 115
   Myths 117
   The Sacred Narrative 120
   What's Wrong With Religion? 121
   Imagination and "Spirit" 125
Chapter 10   Fundamentalism 129
   Theocracy 134
Chapter 11   Summing Up a Life: Family 139
   Souls 141
   Belief 143
   Reality 149
   Creativity 152
Chapter 12   Making Life Worthwhile 155
   First—Perfect Democracy 156
   Beware the Fervor of Religion 157
   Do Something Worthwhile 162
      Planned Parenthood 162
      Habitat for Humanity 163
      The Carter Center 164
      American Friends Service Committee 165
   Making Plans—to Say Goodbye 166
   Conclusions 168

NOTES 173

BIBLIOGRAPHY 183

APPENDIX A 188

APPENDIX B 191

INDEX 192

PHOTO PAGES 79-86

INTRODUCTION

Why would anyone undertake the writing of a memoir? At the risk of demeaning the objectives of those who have written theirs, my reasons are straightforward. As people grow older, sooner or later they will wonder who their ancestors were. Where did they live? What did they do? What did they think about, and accomplish?

My audience is my family and friends. There are no written accounts of near relatives to which I can refer. Thus, it seems appropriate for me to provide a description of my life to pass along to my descendants. I am cautioned about constructing an extensive family tree by the recent article *The Family Tree, Pruned*, by Richard Conniff (Smithsonian, July 2007). He emphasizes that genealogical studies can have rather dubious outcomes—one can find kinships with someone very important or someone very nefarious. The trees of "important" people, such as Thomas Jefferson or Winston Churchill, suggest that "many humble souls born in the immediate vicinity of great families can probably make just as good a claim for a place in the family hierarchy." In fact, a group called the Descendants of the Illegitimate Sons and Daughters of the Kings of Britain does just that. You can look them up at "royalbastards.org." Indeed, if you go back enough generations, you learn that everyone is related to practically everyone else.

Of course, the older one becomes the more memories one accumulates. Fortunately for me, the pleasant memories far outnumber the unpleasant ones. A most significant objective of this work is recalling and recording specific details of incidents and periods of my life. My intention is to verbally revisit places I have lived and some of the places to which I have traveled and describe my impressions and relevant historical events. As the manuscript developed I realized my life had coincided with a significant period of cultural evolution—from *theism* to *humanism*. My curiosity about reasons for this transformation, strengthened by scientific research, led to the realization that my life was a significant replication—an experimental and experiential *sample*—for analysis of cultural events during the last century. Basically this represents an inquiry into origins of life and ultimate biological realities of human behavior.

Aside from any genetic factors that might influence abilities, a child may become aware that various elements exist for self-refinement or refinement of the world in general (e.g., the arts and/or leadership qualities), then learn to understand and appreciate them, hopefully perform or recite them, and, to reach the ultimate degree, actually compose, paint, perform, or otherwise direct the creation of something original. Thanks to my parents, I was exposed to or provided with opportunities for cultural development; I only wish there had been more encouragement and advice. Though I love music, dance, art, poetry, and literature, I have not mastered playing a musical instrument or painting a picture, nor led any significant social or political movement or (aside from scientific publications) written anything of consequence. I still maintain hope that something will develop, as my interests and intentions are extensive.

Many of my ideas and impressions derive from my father's admiration of outstanding leading figures of his time who were noted for their progressive social and political outlook. I realized early on that while he appeared to consider most issues or problems of the world solvable by religious means (i.e., his ministerial profession), in fact his views, hopes, and actions encompassed a broad scope of scientific, political, and humanitarian topics. I was fascinated by the scope of these ideas and the people behind them, and I imagine that that fascination was what later impelled me to focus on and learn about the lives and writings of outstanding thinkers, both past and current. Therefore, this book is intentionally a synthesis of philosophy that will amalgamate ideas of people considered crucial contributors.

My beliefs, as the reader will note in the section on philosophy, are such that I envision no future life or influence, beyond the memory of my experiences and advice that are left for my descendants or other people who may become aware of them. My life may be considered an extremely enjoyable experience, hopefully worthwhile for humanity. Any personal satisfaction of my material accomplishments is far overshadowed by the happiness, development, and success of my sons and their families. As for my posterity, I consider myself simply a crumb in the epoch of evolution of one of the existent species of creatures on a planet called Earth, circling one of the billions of stars of our universe.

Joseph R. Haun
Asheville, NC
October 1, 2011

A Note on Words and Their Meanings

In any book that addresses religious beliefs—whether in support of faith or skeptical of it—certain words carry implications and overtones that either clarify the author's own beliefs and opinions or challenge the reader's—or both. Given my own humanist outlook and the likelihood of a shared atheism, non-deism, or even agnosticism among my readers, my use of certain words is almost sure to raise some people's hackles. Words like "soul" and "spirit" might seem to have no place in the thinking of a scientist or a humanist, but I assert that, in fact, they define, or at least name, certain aspects of the natural world that are just as real as (though much harder to measure than) time and space, or life and death.

Some other terms, like "cultural evolution," can be read narrowly or fluidly; I prefer the latter, if only to reclaim the words from the narrow definitions that constrict them. Evolution, after all, had a meaning of its own long before Charles Darwin appropriated it for biology, and if a species can evolve over time in response to environmental changes as well as occasional mutations or upheavals, so can a society.

Below, then, are a few working definitions that I hope will help readers understand what I mean when I use certain terms. The first two are borrowed from the website www.cultureandreligion.com, which borrowed them in turn from other sources. The definition of "soul" is my own.

Culture is defined as the system of shared beliefs, values, customs, behaviors and artifacts that the members of society use to cope with their world and with one another, and that are transmitted from generation to generation through learning (this definition is from a University of Manitoba web page, selected for its brevity).

www.cultureandreligion.com

Religion is defined as a system of beliefs based on humanity's attempt to explain the universe and natural phenomena, often involving one or more deities or other supernatural forces and also requiring or binding adherents to follow prescribed religious obligations. Two identifying features of religions are they to some extent (a) require faith and (b) seek to organize and influence the thoughts and actions of their adherents. Because of this, some contend that all religions are to some degree both unempirical and dogmatic and are therefore to be distrusted. (This definition is from a Webster's Online Dictionary search for its definition of religion.)

www.cultureandreligion.com

Evolution – "an unfolding, opening out, or working out; process of development, as from a simple to a complex form, or of gradual, progressive change, as in a social and economic structure.

Webster's New World Dictionary, Third College Edition, 1988

Soul is both the most intangible and the most essential aspect of conscious life. Dictionary definitions offer both specific meanings ("the spirit of a dead person…separate from the body and leading an existence of its own"; "an individual person" [*a kind soul*]) and abstractions ("the moral or emotional nature"; "the vital or essential part, quality, or principle" [*brevity is the soul of wit*]; "embodiment; personification" [*the very soul of kindness*]).

Carl Sagan in *The Demon-Haunted World* has listed attributes I would like to think characterize the soul: "All the mammals—and many other animals as well—experience emotions: fear, lust, hope, pain, love, hate, the need to be led. Humans brood about the future more, but there is nothing in our emotions unique to us."

To me the soul is the sine qua non of human existence: it is not only the <u>part of us that makes us wonder</u> about life and death, the world around us, ourselves and others; it is also <u>what we wonder about</u>. It comprises the kinship we feel for other living things—people and animals alike—and is equally the point of origin of the affection animals can feel for us. (Our interdependence with our pets, farm animals, and other mammals is well documented. We and they mourn each other's passing—dogs in particular seem to grieve at the death of a beloved human companion—and elephants have demonstrated some of the behaviors of grieving and even tending to their fallen kin, covering their bodies with leaves and branches.)

"Soul" is, similarly, the <u>self-awareness</u> that causes us from early childhood to consider, "Who am I? How did I get here? Why am I here?"; it is equally awareness of <u>what is beyond our selves</u>: "What is this universe I am part of? Where do I fit into it? Am I but a grain of sand in some vaster enterprise?"

To me it is not in answering these questions that we can define or identify "the soul," but in asking them. Without that intangible part of ourselves, we would not ask, nor would we discover and embrace our emotional ties to other living beings (or, in the case of many, to imagined or hoped-for deities). Our soul lets us feel kinship not just for those who share our close genetic ties, but even for our enemies, in our compassion for the fallen and our regret for lives lost.

Many people think, legitimately enough, that pure intellectual curiosity is enough to motivate discovery and pursuit of knowledge. But that is the work of machines and automatons; we are *Homo sapiens*, the thinking people, who ask questions *simply because we do not know the answers*. Our forebear *Homo habilis* learned to fashion tools, not out of idle curiosity but with a purpose—because they enabled him and his genetic offspring to survive more easily. But *habilis* also *shared that newfound knowledge with others*, ensuring that the larger community could also survive. That genetic impulse, to me at least, is the soul of life.

Unbelievable!

Faith, Reason, and the Search for Truth

The author's Edinburg, VA birthplace, one of several buildings in Edinburg's historic district listed on the state historic register

Faith

This first section, FAITH, recalls the period and process of absorbing the influences of parents, teachers, the environment of my early life, of living under the assumption that the realities governing my life were not subject to question or revision. It describes a time and circumstance when, though questions about the world abounded, the rubric itself remained unquestioned, and unquestionable.

Chapter 1

The Shenandoah Valley

My life began on May 13, 1922 at 105 South High Street, in Edinburg, Virginia. This little village in the Shenandoah Valley is considered one of the most beautiful places to live in the world. My father thought so, and his perspective was surely influenced by his travels through New England, Ohio, and Tennessee. Even such limited travel, just at the threshold of the automobile age, was considered extensive at that time by many of his relatives. Though I lived there only a small fraction of my life, and my perspective has expanded greatly as a result of numerous trips throughout America and Europe, I still find the desirability of this place undiminished.

My numerous summer visits as a child created the impression that life on the farms where my parents were reared was quite grand. The huge Percheron horses, used for essentially all fieldwork, were gentle and fun to ride. My brother and I were pleased and excited to be allowed to help gather eggs and feed the chickens, pigs, cows, and other animals. I still carry beautiful memories of the views of wheat- and cornfields, haystacks, gardens, and orchards. Despite long days of toil, lack of indoor plumbing, and other inconveniences, our relatives seemed to live quite happy and prosperous lives.

My memories of life on these farms were further enhanced by seeing paintings in art museums by John Constable and J.M.W. Turner of almost identical bucolic farm scenes in England during the early nineteenth century. For one with a love for animals and an interest in caring for them it is nostalgic to think of the time when it was possible to do this and still make a living. Unfortunately the advent of modern farming techniques has largely precluded the enjoyment of this aspect of rural life.

Edinburg is located a few miles south of Maurertown, where my mother's (Rhodes) family farms were located. My father also grew up on a farm near there, but his family moved to the county seat, Woodstock, a few years before I was born: my grandfather Haun had given up farming and started to work in a dry-goods store; he also became County Clerk. Since this was before the days of typed records, all the entries were made in longhand, so the clerk needed to have a good bit of skill in penmanship. One can still see his beautiful writing in the old record books kept in the courthouse.

My father, Charles, the oldest of four children, was fortunate to be able to attend college, considering my grandparents' limited income. He, his brother, Ray, and his sisters, Virginia and Elizabeth, did it by way of scholarships, summer jobs, and loans—which plagued them for many years afterward. My father earned an AB degree at the University of Virginia, Charlottesville, and a master's degree at Vanderbilt University in Nashville. He attended Hartford Theological Seminary in Connecticut and became a minister in the Congregational church. At the time of the First World War he went back to Vanderbilt for graduate study and became involved in the YMCA as a chaplain (for military service) at Fort Oglethorp near Chattanooga, Tennessee.

During this period he and my mother were married and survived the great influenza epidemic of 1918-1920. They told me of the multiple funerals that occurred every day during those years. After the war my father went back to Vanderbilt for graduate work and part-time ministry at Old Hickory, Tennessee, where my brother John was born. From there the family moved back to Edinburg, Virginia, where father became a high school principal and part-time minister—and where I was born, fourteen months after my brother.

Several aspects of my father's life in Virginia contributed to my impressions of his interests: his happy early childhood on farms out in the country northwest of Woodstock; associations with his paternal Haun and maternal Wiseman relatives, prominently his uncles Phil and Rob; his aunt Maud Blackwell who lived on the Chesapeake Bay; and his comments about the University of Virginia. He was quite proud of the institution as he showed me the room in which he had stayed, near the one Edgar Allan Poe had once used. He spent much time telling about Thomas Jefferson's design and plan for the school and took me to Monticello on several occasions to admire the beauty and creativity of its design. The heavily underlined pages of reference volumes I later found on our bookshelves made it clear he greatly admired Jefferson. My own interest in the man grew so much in later years that I acquired the Dumas Malone six-volume life of Jefferson.

My earliest visits, beginning when I was about five, were to the original Rhodes farm, where my mother Lydia's two sisters, Rosa and Elizabeth, and three brothers, Carl, Guy, and Ralph, still lived. During this period Aunt Rosa married Uncle Roy (Hockman) and Uncle Guy Rhodes married Aunt Hazel, both moving to their own farms nearby. Ralph also married and chose to stay with his parents, as did Elizabeth and Carl, who never married. Consequently there was ample help for the two-hundred-acre farm, which was inherently labor-intensive. Uncle Carl developed a sizeable orchard with several varieties of apples and became successful enough to purchase a Model T Ford truck, the first motor vehicle owned by anyone in the family.

Since this was in the nineteen-twenties, almost all field operations other than hand labor were powered by horses. To me, as a small boy, it was fascinating to learn by watching my uncles use turning ploughs, mowers, mower-binders, and wagons pulled by two large horses hauling every item or product that had to be moved, whether firewood, hay, sheaves of wheat, manure, or sacks of grain. As there were generally no motors involved, mowers, binders, and manure spreaders were mechanically operated from gears or belts connected to the wheels, which turned as the horses pulled the device.

The use of horses in the early part of the twentieth century is incomprehensible to contemporary readers: there were as many, if not more, horses as people. Their subsequent relegation to minimal usefulness, principally for sport, is one of the results of the agricultural revolution in America. Elimination of the physical and economic burdens of rearing and taking care of horses could be looked upon as a great societal or cultural advancement, except for the fact that a great many people loved their horses more than we do our pets, since they could empathize with the horses for sharing the human burdens of daily life.

On several occasions John and I had fun during wheat harvests. When the mower-binders went through the field they would mow the stalks, bind them with twine in bundles, and leave them scattered through the field to be picked up with a pitchfork. These sheaves weighed perhaps five to ten pounds each, depending upon the moisture of the crop. The wheat needed to be low in moisture for threshing, so the sheaves could be collected with pitchforks and made into piles (shocks) to dry for a few days. As boys we were able to help with this and, later, with loading the dried sheaves on the big wagons to be hauled to the barn. We could ride on the horses or up high on top of the loaded wagons. The process is beautifully captured in Vincent Van Gogh's famous painting of the harvest, "La moisson."

Horse-drawn and/or motor-driven combines had not been developed yet, so it was customary to contract with an itinerant operator to bring in a large, stationary threshing machine to take care of each farmer's crop. It would be placed near the barn or pile of sheaves, so that a line of workers could readily pass them to the steam-powered combine. The grain would spill out of a chute to be caught in buckets or baskets and carried to bins in the barn; the stalks or straw residue would shoot up in the air and accumulate as the big hay-stacks typically seen near barns in farm scenes and pictures of the time, to be handy for livestock bedding in the barn, hen-houses, and nests.

Neighboring farmers would help in the operation at each farm, moving to each location with the hired combine. The women would fix a big meal, served at long tables for men who had washed their hands and faces in pans outside the house. I remember vividly how they looked: the operation was inherently very dusty, so the sweating men would wear straw hats and bandanna handkerchiefs over their noses and mouths as the dust accumulated all over them.

Although it did not make much of an impression on me at the time, the social and religious lives of my relatives and their neighbors was evidenced by the little white church they attended nearby. Outside the church was the graveyard where most of the Rhodes family were buried. The traditions of most of my relatives can probably be traced back to Pennsylvania Dutch[1]. Their Protestant theology seemed to be instilled in everyone as a profound truth that they were expected to accept. Of course, my parents saw to it that my brother and I came along for the Sunday school and sermons during our vacation visits, and, since my father was a minister, he was called upon from time to time to offer a comment or prayer.

Later in life I have often mused about the significance of this religious part of their lives, relative to the many aspects of the work of making a living on their farms. My parents did not try to explain the relationship, nor urge me to learn the details or understanding of Bible stories to which so many references were made. In a sense, this void may be a compliment to them. As they were well educated in philosophical matters, I like to believe that they felt that it would be better for me to form my own opinions about spiritual matters, rather than to insist that I acquire, or passively accept, a memorized knowledge of biblical matters such as their fundamentalist neighbors—and for that matter, most of the country, particularly in the South—held and believed.

My mother, who attended Lynchburg College in southern Virginia, was the only one of the six children of her family educated beyond high school. At that time, it took a degree of dedication even to attend high school, as she had to drive a horse and buggy about seven miles each day to attend her school in Toms Brook.

New England and Pennsylvania

When I was four years old we moved to Columbia, Connecticut, where my father became the minister of a Congregational church. I remember very little of this home, except the general appearance of the Colonial-style house and the typical New England church with steeple and gabled roof.

After only a year or two my father either chose, or was asked, to transfer to a church of the same denomination at Le Raysville, a very small town in northeastern Pennsylvania. From our parsonage we could walk only a few thousand yards to the open country of forest or farmland. It was here that many happy memories of my early life began to unfold. The church and the house in which we lived were very

Charles C. Haun (1921)

similar to those in Connecticut. We had a large lawn and garden where my father grew many flowers as well as the vegetables we ate. A large white rabbit, soft, huggable, loveable, was our favorite pet. John started school there, and I remember well the day they let me go to school with him and his subsequent embarrassment at my "immature" behavior.

A parish church in Connecticut

My mother took me for some nice summer walks out of town into the near countryside. Our refrigerator was the traditional ice-box style, and we regularly pulled a toy wagon across the street to a huge old barn-like structure to get ice, which was stored under thick layers of sawdust to preserve it until more could be cut from the lake and placed there each winter. Another frequent activity was the trip several blocks away to the creamery to pick up a pail of milk.

My recollections of the beautiful wildflowers and fleecy clouds in a blue sky have often reminded me of some of Monet's paintings of similar places. Can you imagine a more bucolic scene, which I cherish as the most delightful of my memories?

Church activities involved the usual dressing in "Sunday best" and attending church next door, where John and I sat dutifully on the front row near our mother, who played the piano while our father accompanied the choir and assembled parishioners on the violin. When available, flowers from our garden were used to decorate the church. The "biblical message" sailed mostly over my head, but remnants must have stuck that later came to me as unbelievable. For example, the Lord's Prayer has stayed with me all my life.

> Our Father which art in heaven, Hallowed be thy name. Thy kingdom come. Thy will be done in earth, as it is in heaven. Give us this day our daily bread. And forgive us our debts, as we forgive our debtors. And lead us not into temptation; but deliver us from evil: For thine is the kingdom, and the power, and the glory, for ever.

(Matthew 6:9-13; King James Version)

But, given my age and my concurrent faith in the tooth fairy, Santa Claus, and other magical powers, I didn't realize the ultimate significance of these ideas at the time. Little did I know that they would be incredibly significant elements in my cultural evolution!

One of the more exciting times was when one of the families in the congregation invited our family to join theirs for Thanksgiving dinner. Since there was a considerable amount of snow on the ground, they came in to town to take us back to their farm in a big sleigh drawn by two huge Clydesdale horses. When I see present-day Budweiser television advertisements showing Clydesdales pulling great sleds while happy music plays, my mind immediately reverts to that day.

A sadder memory of that period was the time when both John and I had to have our tonsils removed, an operation then considered almost routine for all children. We traveled to a hospital in Binghamton, New York, about thirty miles north of our home, and endured much sore-throat suffering. Whether this would have been necessary under present-day medicine is a question, inasmuch as the operation was repeated on me twice more later in life.

Our life in Le Raysville ended when my father was invited to the school of religion at Vanderbilt University in Nashville to teach and develop a program for rural ministers. My assumption is that his many experiences with small rural churches north and south qualified him for this work. As I was only five years old, I had no understanding of some aspects of that work at the time, but in later years I found that, while the overall program was surely a huge success, all might not have been going to his—or some of his parishioners'—liking. Since my early life there was such a happy memory filled with cheerful occasions, I had assumed that it had been a good experience for him as well. But many years later when I asked about it he said it was one of the worst in his life, although he did not explain why. I also learned that he

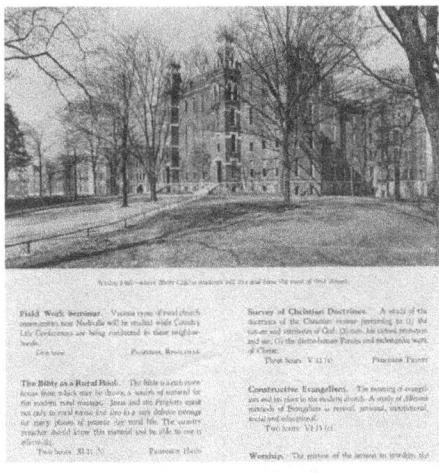

Wesley Hall, Vanderbilt University: Professor Haun's course listing

had promoted the showing of movies (silent in those days) on Saturday nights, an activity frowned on by some in his church.

After Le Raysville we moved many times and many places, but the actual physical process of that relocation has remained in my mind. I describe it here because of the huge contrast with twenty-first-century methods. Our everyday transportation was a Model T Ford with fabric sides for winter weather. Everything had to be packed with lots of wrinkled paper in sturdy wooden boxes or barrels, nailed shut, then hauled by car or truck to the nearest railroad station, twenty miles away. Barrels that were too heavy to pick up were easily rolled by one man up incline boards to the truck (motorized forklift units were not available then, though hand trucks could also be used to push things around.). Moving by freight train took many days, giving the family ample time to journey to the new location.

Nashville

People ask me from time to time, "How did you come to live in the South?" Given my father's unhappiness—and perhaps the congregations' dissatisfaction—with his work in various churches up north, plus his being a Vanderbilt alumnus, I would guess that he was glad to be invited to Nashville. He joined the School of Philosophy and Religion as Professor of Rural Life and Religion, to direct rural church schools, principally for ministers from all over the country.

I had no idea of the magnitude of change from northern Pennsylvania to the middle of Tennessee, both in geography and culture. But of course, it gradually sank in. My folks probably felt it was better for John and me to learn from school and other associations with people, rather than explaining in a way that might bias or prejudice our attitudes. There were no minorities in the segregated school where I started first grade, but of course I did not know the meaning of the word. And I have essentially no memory of the nature of my first lessons, but I vividly recall the outdoor toilets we had to use and the foul aftertaste of sulfur in the

Our first Nashville home

"delivered" drinking water. Our rented house was of nineteen-twenties vintage, fortunately with indoor plumbing, space for a garden, pet goat, dog, cat, and a bit of lawn.

Our place was a few miles out of the city on the main road to Murfreesboro, and as it was the midst of the Great Depression—much worse in the South than in New England—many homeless tramps or hoboes, usually bearded and wearing ragged clothes, passed on foot, knocking on doors for handouts. Most times, my mother would try to find some chore they could be paid for, though we certainly had very little money to spare; if that was not possible, some food or a sandwich would be provided. My parents had great concern for poor people and their economic plight, but since the reasons were not explained to me, I understood only much later in life the dire straits that people endured.

Speech among the schoolchildren seemed foreign to me, especially such terms as "ain't," "nigger," (or "nigga" as it might have been pronounced), and "tater" for potato. My parents quickly corrected grammatical errors, so I later paid too little attention to the required English lessons, making all my later efforts in French and German (required for my PhD) much more difficult. As for the racial terms, John and I were given emphatic instructions to use the word "Negro," although later in the century that word, too, would fall out of favor, replaced successively by "Afro-American," "black" (as in "Black pride"), and today's preferred "African American."

After about a year in Nashville my father found a nice house for sale at the Depression-time bargain price of five

> In my desire to be accepted by my schoolmates, I must confess that I frequently used the forbidden words in those early years (away from home, of course). This led to what I referred to in later life as my "bi-lingual" capability.
> ~ During a prolonged drought you might have heard:
> "Jimmy, yo think it's gonna rain?"
> "Naw, we ain't had no luck prayin'. Have you'ns tried that?"
> ~ Conversation supposed to have occurred between two young boys:
> "How old 'r you?"
> "Don't know."
> "Well, have yo noticed girls yet?"
> "No."
> "You's foe."
> ~ Local expressions listed for tourists on the back of the menu at a local eatery, the Moose Café:
> HAIL – Where the Devil lives
> BOUND – (certain), "If ya don't eat you're bound to get hongry."
> FAR — what you have in your fireplace
> ONLIEST — only one: "He's my onliest son"
> RUNT — No longer of value: "You put too much salt in the soup and now hits runt."

thousand dollars. This was, of course, an impossible sum of money, but since it was a huge two-story house with full basement, big enough to split into two apartments, one of which could be rented to cover the payments, he bought it. Also, it was much nearer his work at Vanderbilt.

At that time and that age (between my second and fourth grades in school), I had limited interest in various things around Nashville, but when I revisited them years later, I realized they had provided significant intellectual enrichment. First of all, the newly constructed replica of the Parthenon[2], built between 1921 and 1931 (the original, of course, in Athens, Greece, was constructed in the fifth century BCE), was not far from where we were living. Our father was fond of pointing out for John and me the many subtle architectural features that counteract one's natural perception in order to be pleasing to the eye, such as the very long foundation steps on the sides that look perfectly level, as you would assume proper construction would be, but in fact are slightly higher in the center than at the ends. On a recent visit we were amazed to discover the 1982 addition of a huge reconstruction of the statue of Athena, the goddess of wisdom, inside the Parthenon. The statue is forty-two feet tall, one of the largest in the western world. It was only by visiting the original Parthenon in Athens during a Mediterranean cruise late in life that I learned just how satisfying, and ingrained, this early knowledge was.

The 42-foot-tall statue of Athena in Nashville's Parthenon

Another place, the Ryman Auditorium, opened in 1892, was the chief civic center location for music and culture. Despite the Depression, my father managed to take the family to a number of historic (and some not so historic) events with seats in the first or second row. John Philip Sousa's band was most exciting, as we sat close to the stage while the huge band played his *Stars and Stripes Forever* and other stirring marches. From the same seats we also enjoyed Ignacz Paderewski, the great pianist and prime minister of Poland (1919), a stunning grey-haired gentleman who played, at center stage, a solitary grand piano.

In this auditorium we also saw some of the early shows of the Grand Ole Opry, which the Ryman hosted from 1943 to 1974. My father was never a fan of country music, but I think he thought of it as a good expression of folk-art, a truly creative endeavor by the "natives" of the area. Admission to—and possibly performers' wages for—these events was either free or very nominal. As well as playing the violin in church, our father had a great appreciation for classical music and arranged for me and John to take three years of piano lessons; thus he presumably wanted us to witness or experience as much music as possible. Sadly, neither John nor I ever became adept at playing any instrument, though I appreciate both classical and popular music and greatly enjoy dancing. Perhaps we were lacking an essential gene. (Our sister Margaret, eight years younger than I, did become a proficient pianist and piano teacher, although she confided to me once that she was tone-deaf and recognized notes by eye rather than ear.)

In those childhood years I did not appreciate my father's concern for improving interracial relations. One family event that I remember, and which I much later realized exemplified his very genuine and personal attitude toward African Americans, was a social visit in the home of James Weldon Johnson[3]. Johnson was a professor of literature and creative writing at Fisk University, the most prominent black university in the country, and the visit might have been for the purpose of strengthening interactions between the two universities. John and I played with his children with no concern for the racial differences, not knowing that this type of social contact was extremely rare, indeed that it was utterly frowned upon by most churches and schools. Fisk was famed for its great choir performances of what were known as "Negro Spirituals." My appreciation of our visit was enhanced in retrospect when I learned that Johnson became quite famous for his writing, poetry, and music.

In reading Johnson's works, I came across a reference, in the preface of *God's Trombones,* to a sermon of my father's titled "The Valley of Dry Bones." In a sudden flashback, I realized I had said as a child sometime, "Your sermon (of the same title) was very interesting," or something like that. I mention this simply to demonstrate that a presentation of this type—a traditional Christian sermon, for example—is an element of cultural evolution that can embed itself in the minds of people regardless of their understanding or lack thereof. Thus do many devout people accept as fact what is, in truth, utterly absurd information about history, life, and the purpose and destiny of mankind, particularly if they are not intelligent or well educated (in some cases even if they are).[4]

Although we lived a few miles inside the city limits, in an area with typically small lot sizes, my father felt impelled, by either the stress of our meager income or a love of farm animals, to have some chickens and a cow. Doubtless there were no zoning restrictions; if there had been I am sure he would have observed them. I also suspect he felt a need to expose his children to the essentials of making a living and/or love for animals. So we suddenly had a nice Jersey cow and several dozen White Leghorn hens and a few roosters. He chose the Jersey because of its naturally high-cream milk, and Leghorns for their relatively high egg-laying traits. There were several vacant lots nearby in which we had permission to stake the cow for pasture—though we had to move the tether peg several times each day. Little did we realize how much "fun" we—and our mother when we boys were in school—were having taking care of these dear family members.

My father's ingenuity or resourcefulness did not stop with this outlandish achievement in the city limits; he also wanted to incorporate a pedigree system of Leghorn improvement to enhance the quality and price of chicks we would produce. Since this was long before the time of scientific hybridization we would use the centuries-old process of progeny selection from individuals with outstanding characters. To do this with chickens you have to be able to identify each individual, which we did by attaching a numbered metal band on one of its legs. A record was made of many features that can be documented: body weight, frequency of molting (when a bird molts it also stops laying), the size and number of eggs each year, longevity of sustained production, etc. The objective was to develop larger individuals, as Leghorns are typically smaller than the meat breeds; larger eggs; and longer production each year.

Our father tried to keep up with university research reports and learned of the discovery that the shortening of days in the fall causes chickens to molt and stop laying. Using electric lights in the evening to lengthen the autumn days greatly enhances the egg production. Also, to accomplish the pedigrees you have to have a system for record-keeping; when you collect eggs from the nests you have to know which hen produced each one. So nests are located on a shelf, each one in a compartment with a trap door that closes when a hen goes in to lay an egg; for the egg to be collected, she must be lifted back out of the cage by hand.

Each egg is marked with the hen's leg-band number and then kept for a period of seven to ten days in a temperature-controlled room. All the eggs from the same hen are placed together in a loose-fitting mosquito-net or thin gauze bag, stapled shut, and placed in an incubator. When the chicks are hatched, they, too, are carefully labeled with a small metal numbered band pierced through the thin web of their wing. This is probably quite painless, as each one is given a sip of buttermilk and then begins to hop merrily around, picking up finely ground food. When they have grown large enough, the wing band is replaced with a leg band to keep for life. Father kept the records, but it was Mother's duty to let hens out of the nests and collect and label eggs two to four times each day when John and I were in school.

I describe all this because it was, perhaps, my earliest exposure to and involvement with the scientific method—a habit of thought that has shaped and influenced my life ever since. Our "fowl-breeding" continued at each of our next residences with the same chickens, so that after a few generations, we could identify distinct changes. The quality of our eggs improved, so that we could sell eggs at premium prices, guaranteed to be from outstanding hens. The business never developed substantially, thanks to our changing family priorities, though the success of the breeding efforts must have been quite satisfying to Father. Perhaps it was fortuitous that he did not live long enough, or was not aware in his older years, to learn of the fantastic results from the science of hybridization. Chickens were bred that could lay eggs nearly every day for long periods, producing more than three hundred eggs per year, whereas we thought a hen did exceptionally well to lay two hundred fifty.

Our school was about five blocks away. There were no school buses, and Father needed to take our only car to work before school began. Mother never had the privilege of learning to drive, so from second through fifth grades John and I walked to school. School life was rather placid—limited moments of glee interspaced with bits of joy in discovery—learning how to add and subtract mixed fractions. I do remember one unhappy episode when I was sent to the principal and spanked for being accused (falsely) of throwing pebbles at a robin during recess.

With chores after school, looking after the cow and chickens, doing homework and piano practice, not much time was left for recreation. The traditions—even the lexicons—of "overnights" or "sleepovers" had not developed in those days, though John or I had occasional friends come to play in the yard or a nearby, and visible, vacant lot; but our lives were definitely structured away from frivolous activities.

The deepening nationwide economic depression was being felt everywhere. Father's work at Vanderbilt finally ended, and he obtained various short-term positions at foundations and public agencies to do sociological studies of unemployed people. One of these, to which he took me along for a week, was in Everets, Kentucky, among unemployed striking coal miners. From the grubby hotel where we stayed we could hear occasional gunfire during the night.

Fortunately Franklin D. Roosevelt's various New Deal programs were being established at this time. Among these the Tennessee Valley Authority was of particular interest to Father; he applied for a job and was accepted, so—after several intermediate stops—we moved to Knoxville.

Chapter 2

The Larger World

At this elementary-school period of my life I had only cursory knowledge of the living conditions in Tennessee and parts of the eight adjacent states. Later I learned that the average annual family income was only a few hundred dollars, with some families subsisting on as little as one hundred dollars per year. Only three percent of farm families had electricity. Soils were completely depleted of nutrients and so eroded by poor farming practices as to be unusable. Most of the timber had been cut, and a huge part of what remained was burned each year to clear more land for farming. Conditions were similar to what we now would consider those of third-world countries.

When I think back to the various events surrounding our move from the North to the South, I remember our having an extended conversation, possibly before my father went to the TVA, but certainly relevant to the Depression, about his motivation and interest in improving peoples' lives. He told me that during his college years he had read about a hero of his—John Frederick Oberlin[5]—who had gone to the Alsace-Lorraine region of France to help poverty-stricken people build roads and develop their farms. Later in life I realized that my father's desire to help might have explained why he was not more satisfied with his experiences in his ministries in New England and Pennsylvania: their people, if not rich, were prosperous enough not to need life-enriching training and social improvement, other than religious activities.

The history of the TVA is based on a unique confluence of geography with several prominent people of the twentieth century. Senator George W. Norris[6] (1861-1944), a staunch Republican who represented Nebraska for over forty years, was the prime source of the idea for the project. After repeated dissapointment with lack of support for his ideas by his party, he joined the Democratic Party, became a friend of Franklin D. Roosevelt, and supported him in his first election as President. Then Roosevelt appointed Arthur E. Morgan[7], H. A. Morgan[8], and David Lilienthal[9] as the first directors of the project. The following description is from the Franklin and Eleanor Roosevelt Institute (www.rooseveltinstitute.org).

> The TVA story begins at Muscle Shoals, Alabama, where the Tennessee River drops 140 feet in thirty miles. This drop in elevation created the rapids or "shoals" that the area is named for, and made it all but impossible for ships to travel further up the Tennessee River. In 1916 the federal government acquired the site and began plans to construct a dam there. The dam was meant to generate electricity that was needed to produce explosives for the war effort, but World War I ended before the facilities could be used. During the 1920s Congress debated over what was to be done with the property. Some members of Congress wanted to sell the dam to private interests. At one time Henry Ford offered to purchase the site and develop a nitrate plant in the area.
>
> Senator George W. Norris of Nebraska led the fight to retain public control over the property. Senator Norris had tried six times to introduce bills for the federal development of the area, which were all defeated by unsympathetic Republican administrations. With the coming of the Depression, Americans looked more favorably to government economic

intervention in the public interest. President Roosevelt—who had a personal interest in regional planning, conservation, the utilities question, and planning—backed Norris' plan to develop the Tennessee River Valley.

On May 18, 1933 FDR signed the Tennessee Valley Authority Act. TVA was to improve navigability on the Tennessee River, provide for flood control, plan reforestation and the improvement of marginal farm lands, assist in industrial and agricultural development, and aid the national defense in the creation of government nitrate and phosphorus manufacturing facilities at Muscle Shoals.

The Tennessee River ran through seven states, through some of the most disadvantaged areas of the South. Perhaps the boldest authority given to TVA can be found in Section 23 of the Tennessee Valley Authority Act, where TVA was given a mandate to improve "the economic and social well-being of the people living in said river basin."

http://newdeal.feri.org/tva/tva01.htm (accessed 9/25/11)

My father's interests and actions were greatly influenced, as are mine, by the ideas and philosophies of statesmen and leaders with progressive ideas for improving society, as well as by the lives of average men and women, particularly the so-called "working man." The many mentions and references my father made regarding his personal contacts with Arthur Morgan and David Lilienthal prompted me to study details of their lives, which have subsequently shaped my social and political views.

A wonderful account of the history of the TVA as well as other great engineering achievements is presented in *Great Projects: The Epic Story of the Building of America, from the Taming of the Mississippi to the Invention of the Internet*, by James Tobin. He writes (and my father would have agreed), "Morgan [Arthur E., former President of Antioch College and well-known Quaker] was perhaps the last survivor of the nineteenth-century Utopian tradition. He was a strange figure, smart but otherworldly, deeply self-righteous, moody, wildly hoping for a perfect world but shy about fighting to achieve it. He had written a biography of the utopian writer Edward Bellamy[10], whose futuristic novel of 1888, *Looking Backward: 2000-1887*, had persuaded millions of idealistic admirers to hope for a well-planned, semi-socialist America."

Bellamy had a vision, inspired by Herbert Spencer[11], that the civilizations of the ancient Incas lived in some sort of socioeconomic utopia. Morgan compares "... the welfare program of the Mormon church, which so far as it goes is substantially like that of the ancient Peru and like the program of *Looking Backward*, the TVA succeeded remarkably and on a large scale."

Morgan saw the TVA as his opportunity to remake society. Soil and farm problems were assigned to Harcourt Morgan (no relation), president of the University of Tennessee, while generating and distributing electricity were the purview of the third member of the board, David Lilienthal, a lawyer and utilities expert.

"The job was immense...and the pace of construction amazed the nation," writes Morgan. High dams in the mountains were for flood-control reservoirs and power, low dams and levees for navigation.

In the early days many poor local residents had a very wary attitude toward these northern liberals trying to tell them about the new things that would be possible through TVA. For decades the giant Commonwealth & Southern Corporation's many electric companies had failed to provide electricity to the region; the company claimed the homes were too far apart and the people too poor to support construction of power lines. The public's skepticism easily transferred to the new company, though as electricity gradually spread through the region the residents became quite loyal to and supportive of the Authority.

The forces of private enterprise, however, did not. Wendell Willkie[12], the likeable president of the giant C&S utilities holding company, became the outspoken opponent of TVA. He championed private ownership of all utilities and wanted the TVA to turn its electricity over to C&S to be distributed to the customers. For some unexplained reason Arthur Morgan, the utopian believer, tried to make this possible, while Lilienthal strongly opposed the idea. He was firm in his belief that it was the responsibility of utility companies to make power available to all people and that they had let the public down. To him, the water flowing in the great rivers, with its power and navigation potential, should be available as a public resource, just as most highways are public rather than privatized.

The men's quarrel became quite heated, and Morgan repeatedly denounced Lilienthal both privately and publicly, until the controversy finally reached the White House. Notes Tobin, "With Morgan defiant in his hatred of Lilienthal, Roosevelt found himself with little choice but to sack Morgan."

Nor was the Morgan-Lillienthal argument the only dispute about TVA. The Authority's very constitutionality was challenged in lawsuits, until the Supreme Court ruled eight to one that it was in fact legal. And Wendell Willkie had enough of a following throughout the nation that in 1940 he ran, unsuccessfully, against President Roosevelt.

It was somewhat of a shock to my father's and my admiration of—even devotion to—heroes to witness the actions of A. E. Morgan, though we never discussed it in later years. It is disappointing to realize that a quasi-believer in a socialist utopia could not support his ideal when it actually arrived, nor anticipate the huge success of the experiment of our government in the TVA. The moral—what I learned from this experience, at least—is that even great persons can have aberrations in their thinking that are seemingly unbelievable in the eyes of others. And, of course, such random events should be expected in the intricate and infinite process of evolution.

The Cumberland Homesteads

Another measure of the success of President Roosevelt's Depression-inspired programs is in the planned community of The Cumberland Homesteads near Crossville, TN. Like the TVA, the project began in the early 1930s as an effort to provide a solution for the grinding poverty and absence of hope among people in the Appalachian region. Many men were working for less than a dollar a day, living without running water, inside plumbing, electricity, and other amenities that are now considered essential in the developed world. The idea was to help these people create a new life for themselves on small subsistence farms—not as an outright gift of the government, but actually in a way that would not cost the government anything. The participants were paid for their work—half in cash, half in "credit-hours"—both to be paid back as long-term, low-interest loans. And of course there were many accusations of "socialism."

> **Butchering a Hog**
>
> A rather sanguine flash-back to the time when we were killing wild animals and butchering hogs came to me recently, not because of the lurid, primitive, or uncivilized nature of it, but because it was so humorous. The University of Tennessee *Farmers Bulletin* offered elaborate instructions for butchering a hog:
>
> *Hang the animal up by the hind legs. Tie his hind legs to the ropes to hoist him up with a block-and-tackle to a large lower limb of an oak tree; then hit its head with a sledge hammer between the ears to anesthetize him; then slit the throat in front of the breastbone, so that blood will drain out of all parts by the time the heart stops (thus enhancing the meat quality).*
>
> We did this by first *catching* the hog from a holding pen without being bitten, though with much slipping and sometimes falling in the mud, along with laughter from me, John, or Dad.
>
> Prior to this operation a large metal barrel filled with water is positioned over a wood fire nearby, so that the hog can be lowered into the boiling water; after sufficient scalding to loosen the hair it is then hoisted out onto a canvas on the ground so that we can all work on scraping the hair off with sharp knives; then it is hoisted up again to begin the meat-cutting part. To remove the inner parts, a slit is made (Father did this) on the underneath side from neck to tail, being very careful that it is not deep enough to cut into the parts to be removed.

Eleanor Roosevelt was, at the request of the president, an observer of and occasional visitor to the project. It was a grand, enthusiastically received undertaking and in principle (with modifications) could offer a viable solution to present-day problems of poverty and inequality.

My father's work with TVA brought him into contact with resettlement projects, to which he was most interested in contributing. He found a position in the personnel division of the Cumberland Homesteads, where his job entailed selecting among applicants from area families in the most extreme need. He also decided that our family would live as homesteaders in one of the homes being built and to participate as much as possible in physical labor and community activities, such as the organization of cooperatives and a community non-denominational church.

The project was located on approximately twenty-six thousand acres of cut-over timberland on the nearly level Cumberland Plateau in central Tennessee. At two thousand feet above sea level, with some slight, gently rolling hills, the well-drained sandy soil was very desirable for a variety of crops. The two hundred and fifty farms that were established ranged from a few acres to as many as a hundred. Steps in creating the community were similar to those used by early pioneer settlers: trees were cut and sawed into lumber; the land was cleared of stumps, then fenced; and finally barns and houses were built. Mules and horses were used, and a great deal of two-man handsaw work was done in those pre-chain-saw days. Cooperative sawmills and quarries were established to provide essentially all the material for barns and houses. Other cooperatives included a general store, cannery, dairy, and medical service. The homesteaders were taught carpentry, masonry, plumbing, and whatever other jobs needed doing. As mentioned above, they were paid for their work in a manner guaranteed to provide pride in creating their own homes and dedication to the project as a whole. The spirits of participants—who for the most part had never experienced such creativity and the anticipation of such nice places to live—were incredibly elevated.

Barns were built first, in which homesteaders lived, mostly without electricity, running water, or indoor plumbing, while their houses were being constructed. My family experienced this phase as well. When we moved into our barn it was like turning the clock back fifty years. But we loved it: for my brother and me, it was like camping out! My father believed that his children should know how to work, as he had, on a farm. We learned to milk a cow, harness a horse, and

---

Well, on this beautiful autumn morning with frost on the ground and everything going beautifully, Father cut slightly too deep, and a strip of feces (commonly known by our school acquaintances as "shit") suddenly appeared on Dad from forehead to waist. John and I naturally couldn't contain a few laughs. However, what was noteworthy was that Father didn't say a single four-letter word, either profane or "polite"—though I am sure this must have been the nearest he ever came to swearing. Of course he had to run for the house to get a bath and clean clothes.

This rather barbaric account is completely out of sync with my current philosophy. Based on the number and types of relationships I have had with farm animals and with pets, most recently our dog Lucas, I believe that they have souls as humans do and therefore should be treated as such. (Such a belief, of course, depends on one's definition of "soul." See p. xii)

And while butchering farm animals is often a decisive factor in a person's commitment to being a vegetarian, I am still eating meat, and the barbaric treatment of animals continues all over the world. But I am grateful for all the animals that have been spared such brutal treatment, and my admiration is unlimited for all the vegetarians and vegans in the world, despite the paradox of "sacred cows" roaming the streets of cities in India while people starve nearby.

butcher a hog. We used a trap line to catch opossums, rabbits, skunks, and raccoons, which we then skinned, and we sold the hides to Sears & Roebuck (this was long before concerns arose about the ethics and the ecological impact of wearing fur).

After about a year we moved into our grand house. It was small by present-day standards, with three bedrooms upstairs, downstairs a study and other rooms, and a nice fireplace. Each homesteader could choose from about six or eight house plans, with a selection of wood paneling throughout the house and partial or complete quarried or fieldstone exteriors.

After the great project was completed, with community activities happily moving along, it gradually became apparent that many of the residents would need an additional source of income. The agricultural revolution was beginning to impact all small farmers. For many decades successful small farming had involved the production of a limited number of plants or animals, but in greater quantities than the farm family needed, and the excess was sold to pay for items not produced on the farm. As mechanization and enormous efficiency gains accrued on large farms, it became clear that hardly any product could be profitably produced on small farms. Consequently, several small industries were recruited to locate nearby. Then the war effort began to take effect and, with considerable distances to commute, many homesteaders found other employment.

A decline in the "community" structure began when some of the occupants decided to move and sell their places. The original objective of helping people in need began to collapse. That situation could have been avoided if the original sales contracts had guaranteed market-level reimbursement to any family wishing to sell its property, so that it could be made available to some other needy family. Still, the project was quite successful: almost seventy years later, more than 50 percent of the homesteads are still owned by original occupants or their heirs.

While the small subsistence-farm model was already becoming obsolete, the Cumberland Homesteads model, if located sensibly with respect to employment opportunities and good transportation, is still quite feasible. It could serve particularly well for the huge fraction of the population that enjoys contact with nature, home gardening, animals, fresh air—i.e., "the simple life."

Chapter 3

Education, Formal and Informal

Looking back, it's apparent that during my first few grades of schooling in Nashville I lacked either the inspiration or the aptitude for learning. Though many things of a basic nature were surely stored in my subconscious mind, my few specific memories are mostly of a non-academic nature. My sole academic memory is of the satisfaction I felt in discovering how to add fractions with different denominators. More prominently, I remember meeting my first girl friend, spending a few pennies for candy in a little store on the way to school, and being falsely accused of throwing stones at a robin, for which offense, though innocent, I was paddled by an ugly, unpleasant, and unforgiving school principal. I recall witnessing a schoolmate at the next desk have an epileptic seizure, learning about sex from another school friend, and taking a detour from the six-block walk to school in order to stroll around the local airport and actually touch the sides of the fabric-covered airplanes of the time.

While crucial elements of my education should have started in what is now called middle school, we moved so many times that I acquired very little substantive knowledge—though undoubtedly the community and socio-geographical experiences were beneficial. Between Nashville, circa 1933, to settling at the Cumberland Homesteads in 1936, we moved five times, including two sojourns at Pleasant Hill, a noted Settlement School[13] founded by religious crusaders from "up north" trying to bring education and a better life to the poverty-stricken South.

Looking back on those early years, I have to have great appreciation and respect for the things my parents taught or showed me, and for the example provided by their lives. They were not, of course, encyclopedic in their teaching: it could be said that they were quite prudish about sex, and utterly oblivious to changing mores with respect to drinking and smoking, let alone gambling.

To my memory there was never a single verbal reference to the subject of sex that was sufficiently explicit to provide a plausible explanation for the biological imperatives of attraction, jealousy, or the structural or behavioral details of sex. Then again, to their credit, they did not substitute archaic or folkloric metaphors such as one I heard a small child at a wedding whisper to his mother: "Mommy, when's he going to put the pollen on her?"

As for smoking and drinking, my parents made valiant, if ineffectual, attempts at proper guidance. In college my brother and I quickly succumbed to both vices, along with penny-ante poker, although later in life I stopped smoking and adopted the medically proven "moderation" in drinking. Our father was vehemently against alcohol, even expounding at length on his participation as a college student in the demonstrations during the nineteen-twenties in favor of prohibition and raids on speakeasies. Both he and my mother were staunch members of the Women's Christian Temperance Union[14], and John and I were taken to some very graphic WCTU slide shows showing the damage smoking causes to the lungs. Evidently this was not sufficient to counter the widespread image of virtually every famous movie star, either as a personal smoker or in depicting the presumed harmless casual smoking of a movie character. It is difficult for me to understand just how our father dealt with the fact that FDR, his social and economic idol, was a "wet," as was Herbert Hoover[15], who had been elected previously on a platform of prohibition—for which I presume Father and all of his (Christian) relatives had voted.

My early education was also somewhat limited by the conditions we faced during high school. At first John and I had to ride ten miles to school in a "school bus"—homemade on the chassis of a truck—that was shared by students from other mountain communities considerably farther away. We attended the only public high school for the entire county, whose teachers had as little as two years of college training. Many of our schoolmates came from one-room schools in the mountains, and their teachers had had no more than high-school educations. Not surprisingly, both John and I failed algebra and had to take it a second time; lacking one of the sixteen credits required for graduation, we had five years of high school instead of the usual four.

Possibly because we were in a "back-to-nature" mode at the Cumberland Homesteads, our father also insisted that we take classes in such manual arts as woodworking and agriculture instead of chemistry, physics, Latin, and other courses that would have helped us in our later scientific studies. Yet despite these obstacles, or perhaps as a result of them, John finished as Valedictorian and I as Salutatorian of our respective classes. Some vindication for having to repeat algebra came later, in college, when I was the only one in my class able to give a blackboard drawing and solution for the Pythagorean Theorem.[16]

I also recall one bittersweet incident from an English class. I had chosen to present an oral report on Sir Walter Scott's classic historical novel *Ivanhoe*. I was so fascinated by his beautifully detailed and involved account of chivalrous English life that I later read *Quentin Durward* and *Rob Roy* as well. In my enthusiasm for *Ivanhoe*, I naturally included every seemingly essential part of the book; later, in private and without a complimentary word, my spinsterish teacher, no doubt impatient to leave for the day, admonished me for taking too much time for the report.

BEREA, KENTUCKY

Throughout our early childhood our parents made many fond references to their associations with educated acquaintances, with the implication that a college education was essential for success, not just to ensure increased earning potential in the future but for intellectual enrichment throughout life. I had a vague notion that they had school debts, albeit with extremely low interest rates, that had hung over them for years. So now, in middle of the Depression, how could we afford college? Our folks did not want us to go to a large university, particularly one with no special academic renown, and a few fruitless thoughts of attending a highly rated place such as Oberlin, Antioch, or Beloit soon gave way to the obvious fact that such small, selective colleges were also unaffordable.[17]

Berea College finally came to our attention. Although initially it might not have been considered by our parents, in part because of the underprivileged nature of the student body, it happily became the school of choice for all of our family. Berea was widely acclaimed for its high academic standing, religious origins, and the fact that all students were required to work for their education—especially important as most of their parents had very limited income. The abolitionist founders as well as later benefactors had planned that the college should serve black students along with white students from the Appalachian region, where most schools were poverty-stricken and substandard. Other factors that must have appealed to our parents, though not discussed with John and me, were the school's strong nondenominational religious underpinnings and its strict prohibition against smoking and drinking.

There was, and still is, no tuition charge at Berea, the result of huge endowment funds that accrued from its noble purpose. (Through substantial gifts to Berea, our families have repaid for our education, paid penance for any transgressions of rules, and helped to sustain the great legacy of the institution.) Students were paid for their labor at rates that, from 1940 to 1943, began at ten cents per hour, with gradual merit increases to twenty cents. That income was applied to room and board, and could, with meager additions by parents, cover all expenses. Students worked in all aspects of operating the college, including the farm, dining room, laundry, maintenance, hotel, candy kitchen, broom factory, and offices, with many of these operations also used for classroom instruction. Students of parents with absolutely no way to provide supplemental funds would have to attend for an extra semester or year to graduate. Despite Berea's austere nature, many gifted professors dedicated their lives to this beneficent institution, whose many prominent graduates and scholars are evidence of the benefit they brought with them.

How could one attend such a place? We were both lucky to have finished high school at the top of our respective classes (in part, no doubt, because the senior classes were so small), and our family's limited income surely helped qualify us. Moreover, our father was known by some Berea authorities for his work to help with the welfare and social improvement of the region, which might have helped on our application papers. In any case, we were both accepted—with the stipulation that our first courses would include remedial English and math.

The first years were dismal, with respect to grades. I did not have a substantive or rational motivation for getting through college. John, my sole guide, gave me much advice plus a system, based on registering for easy teachers, whereby he and others rated them: if you merely attended class you could get a D; if you kept awake in class you would get a C; if you took notes, a B: if you then studied at night, an A. Needless to say, my grade-point average was barely passing. John's was much better, and he was fortunate to discover a great interest in geology and a responsive niche in that department. Later he earned the first PhD awarded by the University of Wyoming and became a noted authority on oil and gas in the Rocky Mountain region.

Among my problems was an excessive preoccupation with girl friends; though not career-advancing, it did lead to me finding my wonderful and talented future wife. Her father was a teacher in the sociology department specializing in recreation studies. Having emigrated from England and studied in Denmark, he was particularly interested in teaching the art of folk and country dancing. That interest led to the formation of a club or demonstration group known as the Berea Folk Dancers, who were asked to do presentations in many places, even, on one trip, in California. My acquaintance with Ruth led to an invitation to join this group. Though probably rather clumsy at first, I managed to fit in with the beautiful, graceful patterns of English dances that used many waltz themes as well as the more boisterous Scandinavian polkas and *schottisches*.

A great point in the enlightenment phase of my life came with a requirement of Berea College for one of two courses in the Bible, studying either the Old or the New Testament. I chose the latter. The rather wide textbook held four columns giving parallel accounts of the four gospels, Matthew, Mark, Luke, and John, with the many major, minor, and missing parts made obvious. Despite its probable goal of scholarly explanation and understanding of the story of Jesus, for me the course simply set the stage for many other considerations of the unbelievable nature of Christianity.

Why was there a need for *four* accounts? Why were there so many differences—if it was supposed to be such a profound document of history?

Above all, with my classes in geology, could such a profound story evolve in just a few thousand of the hundreds of millions of years of the Earth's existence, as documented by undisputed scientific evidence of each of the great geologic ages?

This questioning of conventional Christian truth, particularly with respect to belief that the principal plan for our ethical behavior sprang from the life of Jesus, was justified by anthropological studies I learned about many years later. Nicholas Wade in *Before the Dawn* shows irrefutable proof using modern anthropological studies that include DNA analysis, to validate the evolutionary prehistory of our ancestors. Somewhere between half a million and two hundred thousand years ago, humans had become essentially the same in physical and mental characteristics as they are today. Their—our—propensity for altruistic social behavior also started somewhere within that time frame. In light of that scientific research, the claim of modern religious fundamentalists, indeed of most recognized religions, that belief in their ideologies is necessary for ethical behavior, is utterly unbelievable.

Various comments from students taking the alternate Old Testament course led me to entertain similar conclusions casting doubt of its rational validity. How could the concept of "original sin" suddenly appear in the long evolution of humanity? Moreover, how could Eve's eating an apple from the tree of knowledge accomplish this phenomenon? Whatever the possible metaphor that religionists may assign to this feat, it certainly implies that participating in, or enjoying, fruits of knowledge could be utterly and permanently damaging to one's well-being, particularly in the afterlife. This type of unbelievable information is surely what fuels current "science vs. religion" conflicts in which fundamentalists try to keep the study of evolution out of schools—or at least relegated to the status of "an unproven theory."

Cadet Joseph R. Haun, 1942

Chapter 4

World War II

My college experience was interrupted by World War II, after which I returned with Ruth—whom I had married, while on leave in 1945, in the chapel at Berea—to finish college, with perfect grades, and then to graduate school to earn master's and doctoral degrees.

During those first years of college the news from Europe was grim, with particular implications for those who faced the prospect of being drafted into the armed services. In retrospect many things can be concluded from the events that evolved. Whatever the basic moral implications were, I'm proud of my efforts and at the same time sad for the many friends and wartime acquaintances who were killed or seriously injured.

Like the vast majority of young men who became involved, I had yet to develop mature judgment. Many of us concluded that to join up and be patriotic was better than being cowardly; also, we were certain that eventually we would all be drafted anyway, with universal conscription in effect. By the time I enrolled at Berea, only a handful of male students remained there and in all other colleges and universities. My father, as a minister, had chosen intentional noncombatant involvement during WWI by working with the YMCA; he suggested I become a conscientious objector, which at the time carried the distinct possibility of serving time in prison. Several acquaintances from Quaker families, who were committed pacifists, were given the option to serve in noncombatant activities, their pacifism recognized and honored by the government.[18] But I was not a Quaker, and I had no deep personal moral commitment to pacifism—nor did the prospect of prison appeal to me.

When, midway through college, I learned that a Reserve Officer Training Corps program was available, I was eager to participate. The program empowered the government to offer colleges and universities that lacked ROTC programs a fast way to train officers. Depending on how much regular college one had already completed, training could take as little as three months for line officers—much longer for the air forces—instead of the four-year period for those from the prestigious service academies at West Point and Annapolis.

Berea had such a program for the Navy, and being an officer appealed to me far more than becoming an instant enlisted man with no further college, so I joined the Naval Reserve and continued in school. While hoping that I would not be called to active training before completing college, I learned I might qualify for the Naval Air program: if I could pass the more rigorous physical requirements, I could become both an aviator and an officer. I set forth for St. Louis, Missouri, and despite borderline visual acuity, I passed the tests. The prospect of being a pilot and flying inspired me greatly in those next uncertain waiting days, but my hopes of finishing college before going to war were dashed when my call to duty came just a few months later in 1943.

Ground School

One learns quickly in military training—how to march, obey orders, keep clothes neat and quarters tidy, use guns, survive in countless desperate situations, and many other skills. Somehow the Navy had a way of "outdoing" the Army. Possibly it is more dangerous to fly over water than land—certainly navigation can be much more involved. In any case, my buddies frequently thought the training a little sadistic. Most of the physical training was accomplished with Marine

Corps personnel, well known for their discipline, "spit and polish," and esprit de corps. Naturally, many of my classmates chafed under this regime, but I found the neatness, sense of order, unity of purpose, cooperation, and camaraderie most appealing. The required exercises and sports were rigorous, the food very good; lights out and quiet brought adequate rest, so that everyone felt great; we even gained weight, though not too much because of the strenuous exercise. Everyone had to pass very demanding tasks of timed running and swimming, for both speed in the short distances and endurance for the longer, such as the four-mile run, obstacle courses with ropes and walls to climb and ditches to jump, the two-mile swim, and staying afloat for two hours with nothing but a pair of pants and shirt for flotation.

This schooling took place at various colleges and military bases, including Murray State Teachers College in Kentucky, Arkansas State Teachers College, the University of Georgia, Millington Field at Memphis, and, finally, the Naval Air Base at Pensacola, Florida. Some classroom studies continued at several sites, and we pursued expertise in such essential skills as Morse code, plane and ship recognition, and navigation wherever we went. We learned and memorized Morse code, then listened to it faster and faster to be able to qualify at the required minimum speed. Images of all American and foreign planes and ships had to be learned by rote and then recognized when flashed for one-hundredth of a second on a screen in a dark room. Needless to say, these skills required much practice.

Aside from the flying skills that had to be mastered, celestial navigation was probably the most challenging and, for me the most interesting, of all subjects. We learned the basics of map- and chart-reading along with precise drafting of data received by radio compass, Loran, and astronomical tables of star locations (we had to know the major stars and their constellations). We practiced making simulated flights such as San Francisco to Guam, listing the stars that would be visible (providing the night was clear) for a given calendar date, then selecting appropriate volumes, from the many thousands of Winkletablen charts,[19] to take along. We would apply to those charts sextant or octant readings during the trip, plus the accurate time of night, to determine our exact latitude-longitude position. We also had to deal with a wide variety of complications on an actual trip, such circumstances as unsteadiness of the plane while making octant readings, speed and wind drift of the plane during readings and drafting, and the time elapsed since last readings. With these skills, it was possible to get close enough to destinations to make visual contact and land. Sadly—or perhaps happily—all this sophisticated training is no longer necessary with our present Global Positioning Satellite systems.

Flying

Probably every child has perceived a bird in flight for the first time and pondered, "How do they do it? How great! If only I could fly!" The wing-flapping might explain most of the aerodynamics, but how about the majestic soaring and gliding of buzzards, hawks, and sea gulls?

There was a huge disconnect in my mind between how birds fly and the reality of airplane flight. As with so many of nature's mysteries, the scientific discovery of Bernoulli's principle[20], which explains the principles of lift, and its exploitation with the airplane wing would make possible another of the unbelievable achievements of humankind. Because the Navy wanted to pack as much information as possible about flying into all of its pilots, our courses contained all sorts of details, including the physics of Bernoulli's principle.

Weather patterns and systems were also, understandably, an immediate and constant concern in flying, and were therefore an ongoing feature of our training. "Aerology," as they called meteorology, included basic elements—Earth's rotation, trade winds, ocean currents, cloud types and their meanings for weather predictions—along with freezing rain, storm-tornado-hurricane features, and many other things that probably seemed tedious to many students but were fascinating to me. In fact, the Navy's ground training and flight training were so much more comprehensive than the Army's that it was possible at the end of training for some of our graduates to switch services and obtain the higher rank of First Lieutenant in the Army Air Corps instead of that of Ensign, as usually obtained in the Navy.[21]

Actual flying began at the second base I was assigned to for instruction, Conway in Arkansas. The Piper Cub[22], widely known by then as the most elementary vehicle for pilot training, was my first taste. When my dream of flying became a reality it was exhilarating—soaring about like a bird from a few feet to thousands was everything I had imagined. We performed various strenuous, even dangerous maneuvers in this flimsy, underpowered plane (compared to current aircraft), including a "dead-stick" landing. After what my instructor felt was sufficient training to trust me to land the plane, one day on a landing approach with trees and power lines between us and the field, he suddenly turned the engine off (it had no electric starters) and told me to land it. With a still propeller in my view and a big leap of my heart rate, I did it. (Of course the instructor could have taken over, assuming I didn't freak out and freeze on the controls.)

The fun really began at Memphis, TN, in intermediate training in Steerman and N3N biplanes. Complicated aerobatics, precise two-and-a-half-turn spins, slow rolls, snap rolls, landing in specified circles painted on the ground in remote fields with woods all around—that kind of flying was really exciting! Many of the instructors were civilians recruited from stunt-flying and crop-dusting companies and thus adept at violent and low-level maneuvers. Spins with many fast turns could bring you close to blacking out as the blood left your eyes; inverted spins could bring you close to red-outs as the blood rushed into your eyes. Open cockpits like those of World War I planes let us young pilots really identify with

First flight school, 1942

birds as we darted into and around the edges of great clouds, maneuvers that were forbidden by regulations because of frequent violent turbulence that could sometimes overwhelm your control system—but who knew when you were solo? Broad seat belts had to be kept tight at all times, particularly when flying inverted in various acrobatics, and we all wore, and sat on, parachutes. One of our classmates did fall out of his plane but parachuted safely to the ground; known for some clownish antics, he was suspected of doing it on purpose, and later he was "washed out" of the program. His instructor, sitting in the front cockpit, must have been pretty upset on looking in the mirror, but it was exciting for me, secretly hoping I could jump someday.

The next base, University of Georgia, offered only ground school and physical training. I cherished participating in impressive parades in full dress uniform accompanied by stirring band music, then massed over the entire field for review in the great Georgia football stadium, followed by addresses by admirals and ace pilots on leave from active duty in Europe or the Pacific. On one of these occasions, while massed at attention, we had a low roaring flyover by the Navy's celebrated acrobatic planes, the Blue Angels. They came in tight formation, descending from a very high altitude as if they were actually going to hit the stadium; suddenly, at only a few hundred feet, they turned upward and away in a succession of rolls. The collective thrill of a thousand cadets was dampened only by the Admiral's admonition: "Remember—if you don't do well in your classes, this is the closest you'll ever get to combat flying."

The Pensacola, FL, U.S. Naval Air Station was our final training site. It had multiple fields many miles apart for all the main categories of subsequent service: instrument training, sea planes, fighter planes, multiple engine training, plus a few to simply train in a variety of plane types. After training in various fields I finally opted for multi-engine specialization at Corey Field, and following graduation to officer status and receiving my gold wings (the Army's were silver) I was recruited as an instructor. This was fortunate, as cadets were not permitted to be married, and I was finally able to marry my college sweetheart, Ruth; I was free to bring her to Pensacola, while many of my graduating classmates went immediately to active combat zones.

The chief plane we used was the Beechcraft, a twin-engine, seven-passenger commercial plane, the Cadillac of private planes at the time. Though it was considered relatively safe compared with the much more powerful and faster fighter planes, which had frequent accidents, there were stressful moments in some of the low-level maneuvers. In fact, a former instructor of mine and three students in his plane were killed in an unexplained accident while I was at Corey. My students were seasoned pilots, mostly from active combat in the Pacific, where they had flown single-engine fighters.

Multi-engine planes had some unique characteristics that needed to be understood and practiced; our students were presumably being groomed to fly the newly designed Grumman twin-engine fighter, the F7F Tigercat. One of the most dangerous emergencies that could occur was the possibility of an unexpected pause (or failure) of the lower engine in a turn near the ground. If the pilot did not react instantly with rudder and aileron action, the plane would turn over and crash into the ground. When sitting side by side (student in the left "pilot" seat, instructor in

A Beechcraft training craft: "The Cadillac" of private planes

the right "co-pilot" seat), the instructor could test the student's reaction time in a turn at high altitudes by slyly finding him glancing out the window and, without his noticing, quickly changing some engine control switch or lever to cause a sudden loss of power in the lower engine. Of course, if he didn't react quickly enough, the instructor could make the necessary correction. This procedure became much chancier and more hazardous when tried at low altitudes such as near landings.

Despite some occasional excitement, my life as an instructor was very pleasant, flying four-and-a-half hours with three students each day (weather permitting) and spending a lot of time on the beach or in the officers club. At one point I had been instructing a Marine officer who came from Pacific active duty in landing procedures, and he had made some incredibly hard landings. He also taxied too fast, which I explained was very detrimental to the brakes—but he was in no mood to take a lot of teaching from a naïve kid ten years younger. On a final approach to the runway, the way to check that the landing gear is down is by trying to see just a little bit of tire down past the front edge of the wing. On this occasion, he was looking out the left window to verbally report he "had a wheel," and I looked for the other wheel. Nothing! I quickly aborted the landing and we climbed to good altitude to find the problem. He acknowledged his was not there, although he thought he had seen it. We tried to lower the landing gear using the manual crank, both with and without the electrical activation, but while pulling out of an almost vertical dive it was impossible to get the gear down. We flew low over our control tower so the field commanding officer could watch with field glasses; by radio he told us that the gear was evidently down only slightly and stuck there.

My heart raced, hoping he might tell us to abandon ship and jump—just as I had fantasized earlier. No luck. "Make a careful approach, come in low and slow, full flaps, just over the trees—we'll have fire engines and emergency equipment on hand." I did what he said, and when the propellers bit the pavement with violent vibration, sparks and smoke flew from the runway as we slid to a stop. Fortunately there was no fire as we scrambled out the door to get away as fast as possible, earning a big ovation from a few hundred crewmen and cadets who observed the safe ending to what could have been a catastrophe.

In the spring of 1945 the European war came to an end, then later that year the Pacific war ended. In only a few months we were able to return to Berea, where I would be able to continue college under the GI Bill of Rights program.

World War II led to a great deal of soul-searching, framed (for Americans, at least) by the bookends of the conflict. First came the unprovoked Japanese surprise attack on Pearl Harbor, which in addition to taking eighteen hundred lives directly led the United States into the war. And at the end came the discovery and public disclosure of the German concentration camps with their inhuman, unbelievable devotion to the destruction of human life. In this sense, the war was for valid reasons—certainly not for conquest and territorial gain or for domination and destruction for its own sake.

The war also led to the formation of the United Nations, which should be the ultimate arbitrator of world problems, but our country failed to maintain its responsibility in the operation and success of this organization. This was caused by the politicization of the basic principles that underlay its organization: while most Democrats favored an outgoing regard for other countries' welfare and welcomed the prospect of a harmonious, democratically governed world in the future, many of America's Republican leaders leaned toward greed and/or selfish protectionism.

Chapter 5

Graduate School

Credits for Navy training in mathematics, meteorology, and navigation were transferable electives for my college requirements, so upon my re-enrollment it took me only one semester to graduate from Berea. With the GI Bill available for another three years of higher education, it was almost unthinkable for anyone, particularly from an "educated" family, to do other than continue in graduate school. At the time, sadly, I had no burning desire for any particular profession. Predictably, though, with my AB major in geology (having copied John's sincerely chosen field), I applied for graduate school at the University of Chicago and was accepted. Ruth and I had essentially no savings, but support from the GI Bill ($90 per month, tuition and textbooks paid) and her job in the University administration offices made possible a semester, though we had to live in a rather depressing apartment six blocks south of the campus. Although I made respectable grades and had the good fortune to have as a chemistry teacher T. R. Hogness, one of the noted scientists on the highly secret Manhattan Project that developed the atomic bomb, I gradually developed the uncomfortable feeling that, relative to my interests, perhaps I was not headed for a particularly desirable career.

In search of a way to prepare for continued graduate study in some other field, Ruth and I concluded it might be best to return to Berea for some other basic course preparation. In addition to the regular Bachelor of Arts degree, a BS in agriculture was offered. Being familiar with so many phases of agriculture in my early home life, I thought I could at least become a professional teacher of agriculture for high schools, so I plunged into study.

The basic courses—botany, genetics, horticulture—fascinated me and revealed my preference for biological rather than physical science. To amplify this interest I quickly chose a plan to find a place to do graduate work in horticulture. I applied to several noted schools in this field and accepted an offer to go to the University of Maryland with an assistantship position to supplement the GI bill. Ruth found a nice position in the library, and we enjoyed a comfortable life for the next four years. After a few months living in a rather depressing apartment, twenty-five minutes by bus from the campus, we bought our first car—a six-year-old, four-hundred-dollar, two-door Ford sedan that needed another four hundred to get into safe condition. We then moved to a much nicer one-bedroom government housing development.

Political Awakening

During college and graduate school, our concerns were so concentrated on immediate study for classes, domestic demands, and getting ready to make a living that few of our thoughts involved the state of the nation and who was in office. The great euphoria of the New Deal had been tempered and largely dimmed by the horror and success stories during the war. Thousands of veterans were incredibly grateful for opportunities to go to school under the GI Bill or get employment through other post-war legislation. Other programs spawned by Democratic initiatives included Social Security, a Minimum Wage Law, the Agricultural Extension Service, the forty-hour work week, Workers Compensation, Soil Conservation Act, Unemployment Compensation Act, Rural Electrification Act, Federal Deposit Insurance Corporation, and many other improvements to the lives of American families. When President Roosevelt died, Harry S Truman, largely underestimated as a statesman, continued to implement and enhance programs already in place.

However, as the next election approached, Republican propaganda suggested that the country had somehow slipped into such a "socialistic" or "anti-freedom" condition that we must change course for the betterment of future generations. The popular governor of New York, Thomas E. Dewey, was nominated to oppose Truman.

Public opinion, as indicated by many polls, showed Truman as very unpopular (with essentially zero charisma, even among Democrats) and Dewey virtually unbeatable. Ruth and I had become acquainted with a number of friends who were staunch Democrats, a party with which we could readily identify. On the evening of Election Day we were invited to a party of the faithful. As the evening wore on the news was grim: Dewey had a commanding lead, and near midnight we decided "it was all over" and went home to bed. The next morning, to our incredulous surprise, we learned that Truman had won, and the president had great fun holding up the newspaper headline trumpeting his defeat.

The famous photograph from the *Chicago Tribune*

The Truman era was hugely significant in the development of the United States, and the world, after the war, and its politics reflected both the good and the bad of the time. Zachary Karabell's exciting, humorous and poignant book *The Last Campaign* captures the mood of the time and offers a valuable overview of crucial history in the twentieth century.

It was at this time that I went to work for the E. I. DuPont Company, as discussed in more detail in the following pages. Since many great corporations of the past have been aligned with the Republican Party, it should have been no surprise to me that this company would be also. I was very naïve, but also sensible enough not to engage in work-related involvement in political or religious matters. But my admiration for the company and for my immediate supervisor (later to become Governor of Delaware), who was a superb administrator and friend, caused me to feel secure that they would ultimately do what is best for the country. We also, of course, enjoyed our life and security and did not want to rock the boat.

Still it was evident in various research personnel meetings, country club celebrations, etc. that the "proper stance" would be to support Dwight Eisenhower (the Republican nominee) in the next election. The Democratic Party had the good fortune to nominate Adlai Stevenson, an astute intellectual with incredible experience and qualifications, who we felt could easily defeat the popular general and leader of Allied Forces in WWII. Sadly, Stevenson lost to Eisenhower not only in 1952 but again four years later. This deplorable display of the public's intellect had a depressing effect on my faith that progressive, liberal principles would be recognized essentials of our "informed" voters. However, due to my subsequent employment in the government, with its prohibition against political activities, my own efforts toward changing the situation with appropriate activism would not emerge until much later.

Plant Science

My chosen area for specialization within the broad field of horticulture was mineral nutrition of the geranium plant, more specifically the nutrient influence of the mother plant on the rooting of cuttings, as this was a principal commercial means of propagating unique varieties (and many other species of plants as well). My plants were grown in water-culture containers (today's hydroponics) in the greenhouse so that the chemical composition in each unit could be carefully maintained and monitored, without the confounding effects of compounds and natural organisms found in soil. The procedure for growing plants in solution culture, mostly for research purposes, had been practiced for years. In more recent times the procedure has actually attained commercial significance for highly specialized situations. At the time I did not suspect that this procedure would be my chief research tool for PhD research, or one I would utilize for many years in continued professional research positions after graduation. My work on geraniums, published in a professional journal, showed that the nutrient balance in fertilization could actually be advantageously modified to produce improved rooting, thus offering a contribution to commercial production.

For the past few decades, and especially today, "organic" gardening and farming has been the rage. Aside from various obviously advantageous aspects of this ideology, there has grown a massive misunderstanding that implies that essentially all inorganic chemicals are unhealthy for plant and human consumption, that some are even poisonous. This is a colossally unbelievable proposition that continues despite research confirming that fruit eaten from plants with mineral nutrient elements supplied entirely from chemists' shelves is exactly the same in composition and nutrient value as fruit grown in conventional soils. Of course many chemicals, both nutrients and pesticides, are used improperly and/or in excessive amounts, resulting in a variety of ecological problems—but those are different problems that can and should be dealt with appropriately, not by banning inorganic chemicals.

With respect to insecticides, fungicides, nematicides, and seed treatments, many chemical products invented during the last century have had incalculable value in lowering costs of production, improving the quality, nutritional value, and disease protection of plants, animals, and humans. Providing they have been used properly, many actually degrade to inert substances or totally disappear as physical entities[23]. Nevertheless, the absurd notion persists of a "uniquely vital" quality of organically grown foods and animals. Ads appeared recently even for "organic" cigarettes.

Required courses for the master's degree in horticulture included many taught in the botany department—plant morphology, pathology, taxonomy, physiology, and plant biophysics and biochemistry. My interest and outstanding grades led to an invitation from the botany department for me to continue graduate work with another assistantship position in plant physiology, subsequently leading to my PhD. My research project, a determination of whether copper was essential for plant growth in certain commercial crops, was coordinated by the Battelle Memorial Institute which, not surprisingly, was funded by three major copper companies: Phelps Dodge, Kennecott, and Anaconda.

My use of water-culture methodology to demonstrate the essentiality of copper for plants was rather complex, in that all containers, water, and chemical nutrients supplied had to be "free" of copper. Since copper is a commonly present trace property or contaminant in most things, all my containers had to be especially constructed, water specially distilled to be copper-free, and chemicals obtained without copper impurities. In addition to my successful documentation of the essentiality of copper—in minute amounts—for normal plant growth, I also conducted field experiments across the Chesapeake Bay on the eastern shore of Maryland, where the almost pure sandy soils are notoriously low in mineral nutrients, and demonstrated that additions of copper could be beneficial in crop production. However, it is doubtful that my findings ever had much practical significance. The trace occurrence of copper in most soils, and in commonly applied nutrient materials, negates the use of supplemental amounts and, when needed, can be supplied in fertilizers in such microscopic amounts as to be utterly insignificant from a commercially profitable standpoint. This seemingly negative phase in my research experience was nevertheless an enjoyable application of the techniques for studying the inner workings of living things. Also, expertise in hydroponics was essential in my professional positions after graduation.

DuPont

In 1950 Dr. Hugh Gauch, my professor of plant physiology, contacted the E. I. DuPont Company in Wilmington, Delaware to see if they needed a plant physiologist. They were currently interviewing for such a position in the Grasselli Chemical Department and invited me to Wilmington headquarters. Lavish entertainment and extensive interviews were followed by the offer of a position; later I learned that they selected only one in about fifty of those interviewed.

DuPont wanted someone who could evaluate various candidate chemicals for plant applications, principally as herbicides but also for other pesticidal or fungicidal applications. (The candidate chemicals were identified by their staff chemists.) My knowledge and experience with solution culture seemed to be an ideal means for this research, because potential chemical pesticides could be introduced into the solution culture medium without the buffering and compounding of ordinary testing under soil and/or field conditions. Organic chemicals typically found by screening or synthesized in the laboratory are frequently large, incredibly complicated molecules, often expensive to manufacture. Thus, it is desirable to find the best isomer or analog form of the compound. Chemists created a variety of related compounds, possibly varying widely in either cost or effectiveness, or both. My work with substituted urea herbicides identified the compounds that combined best use with most efficient cost; thus, even if a given candidate might be twice as costly as another, if it was effective at less than half the dosage, it could be selected for manufacture.

One very interesting period of experimentation came when we studied plant metabolism of candidate herbicides, selected for their toxicity, to see if the plant actually absorbed or decomposed them. This information could then be used by chemists in finding other useful related compounds or to attempt modifications of the compound under study. Our technique was to place radioactive carbon (C-14) at various positions in the (usually very complicated) molecular structure of compounds during their synthesis in the laboratory. The "doctored" compounds would be added to the nutrient-solution cultures in which the test plants were growing. Since plants, like animals, emit carbon dioxide in their respiration, and absorb carbon from the air in the well-known process of photosynthesis, we could capture the C-14 by growing the plants in enclosed chambers and then circulating the air through absorption columns that could be later analyzed for the quantity of radioactive carbon. Thus, comparative rates of emission and quantities of C-14 from test compounds labeled in different places in the molecule could be utilized in the search for better products.

Working for the DuPont Company was truly a memorable experience. Its outstanding history of benevolent employee management practices and useful commercial products extends back to the first days of our country. In 1951 William S. Dutton, chronicler of the company, related this history:

> "In 1802, Eleuthère Irénée du Pont de Nemours, refugee from a French dictatorship, established near Wilmington, Delaware, a factory for the manufacture of gunpowder [essential to the United States at that time]. It was a means to life and to the national growth.... DuPont's descendents, carrying on the business in an unbroken line, pioneered in introducing dynamite to the roaring America in the [1880s]. Quickened progress in the fabrication of steel, the building of railroads, skyscrapers and highways soon made the United States the Wonderland of nations."

Despite the fact that their production of explosives had to be split among two competitive companies, because of Sherman anti-monopoly regulations, the company has continued to expand. "Today, the DuPont name is attached to thousands of chemical products, many of which are wholly new to man or nature… and are affecting a revolution more significant to mankind and its future than any ever promoted by drums and gunpowder."

From the company's earliest days it was tireless in stressing the safety and welfare of workers. Relics of the early factories along the Brandywine River in Delaware show how rooms for operations were built on three sides of masonry with one wooden wall facing the river, so that in case of an explosion it could blow out in the river and be isolated from the other operations. Further, only one or two employees were to be on duty in these compartments at any time. Inevitably a few accidents happened in this inherently dangerous business, and in these cases, the injured and their dependents were taken care of for life.

This legacy continues, and the company has an outstanding safety record, even though the chemical industry is noted for exceedingly dangerous manufacturing operations. Even in my office and laboratory environment I was supplied with free safety shoes, clear and tinted prescription safety glasses, and clothes and other protections from chemicals or radioactive substances. Further, laboratories were equipped with all the latest, most advanced technologies available. (In addition, research personnel had the opportunity to belong to a lavish country club for $6 per month with all the amenities, including three 18-hole golf courses.)

The Turning Point

After seven years of marriage, always anticipating that we would have children someday, Ruth and I thought that our income was finally sufficient to begin a family. Within three years Alan and Steven were born and we acquired a small two-bedroom ranch house, with fireplace, in an attractive new development in Newark, Delaware, a seventeen-mile commute from my office in Wilmington. From early childhood I had been an inveterate "do-it-your-selfer," mostly because we never had any money, but also because of a chronic curiosity to learn how things are done. I did all the landscaping, mostly transplanting things from the forests nearby, built an acoustic wood fence around our little back yard, and took care of all maintenance, including car repairs, tune-ups, and oil changes. This attribute was to serve us well over many years in enabling us to build two homes offering accommodations that would never have been affordable otherwise.

As Ruth and I began to raise a family we anticipated that our young children would face problems from their school companions with reference to churches. We remembered our classmates' comments and our own feelings of despair when we couldn't identify with the frequent announcements that "I'm Baptist" or "I'm Catholic"—statements that recurred so often that any normal person would conclude that they, too, should identify themselves as belonging to some religious group. Consequently, we decided we had to try to find the right way to provide for the boys' "social well-being."

How to do this? Join a church? Our whole lives flashed back to relevant memories. There was, of course, our limited knowledge of history, both about various denominations and, more particularly, of the anthropology or cultural evolution of religion. A huge spectrum of possibilities emerged, from the apparent success of Mormonism across the usual litany of Protestant denominations to numerous 1950s cults and sects[24] such as Scientology and Dianetics (and similar precursors of the later "Moonies," Hare Krishna, "Peoples Temple," "Branch Davidians," and countless others).

We also acknowledged the possibility that the success of many religions derives from the lemming-like nature of humans. Superimposed on this likelihood is the fact that vast numbers of people who rarely go to church still readily accept, and even trade on, the assumption—an impression from cultural evolution—that there is a deity that created everything. We also had to deal with the inevitable, indelible impressions, or perceptions, of religion in our minds: lovely hymns in beautiful churches, congenial people, imagined after-death consequences, plus the constant efforts of friends, including one of my professors and a fellow student in graduate school, to proselytize people recently moving to a new location.

After accepting trial periods in several churches we had the good fortune to visit, and subsequently join, a congenial Unitarian[25] congregation, where we were astonished by the rational, ethical, and humanitarian subjects that were addressed. Rather than unending biblical dialogue or the unbelievable doctrines harped on in other churches, the general tenor was concern about current societal problems, and the focus was on actions we could undertake toward improving people's lives and the environment. There was also a positive interfaith attitude aimed at ameliorating prejudices toward, and among, other denominations: one of the children's Sunday school classes was entitled "The Church around the Corner," where students visited

Catholic, Jewish, Moslem, and other faiths' religious services.

From this point on, and for the next fifty years of travel, study of history and philosophy, and associations with free-minded people, my horizons of humanist ethical values were steadily enlarged. My father visited us occasionally, came with us to the Unitarian meetings, and was also much impressed with their social, ethical, and political outlook. Later when I read about the Transcendentalists[26], Thoreau, Emerson, and others (idolized by some Unitarians), and discovered the similarities with Congregational beginnings in New England, I wondered why he had not made some philosophical comment.

Reason

While my education as described in the previous few chapters included both unfortunate elements and much valuable knowledge gained, I continued learning far beyond and long after school. The real development of my intellect begins here, after my formal education ended, as, on my own, I applied rational thought, rather than received understanding and expectation, to what I encountered in my life. Perhaps my own gradual enlightenment will echo, in some manner, the eighteenth-century era of that name, from which we all benefit daily.

Chapter 6

Baltimore Interlude

The first of two great enigmas in my life came after about four-and-a-half years with the DuPont Company. My professional progress, income, lifestyle, family happiness, and security were beyond reproach, yet a yen for "greater things" somehow hatched in my psyche. In retrospect, and in light of later knowledge of subsequent events, my decision to leave this idyllic situation was quite irrational, as substantively based as Yogi Berra's remark, "When you come to a fork in the road—take it."

My rationale was an outgrowth of my years of work on developing a successful chemical product (herbicide) for the company and a desire to actually use it commercially for personal satisfaction and financial gain. I joined a very successful but fledgling pest control business run by former graduate school classmates specializing in entomology. Their company catered principally to larger food manufacturers, warehousers, and handlers, as well as prominent restaurants. The plan was for me to expand their domain by developing a weed control division, principally for industrial sites that required total weed and plant eradication for fire prevention, rodent protection, and ballast protection on railroad embankments. Of course, "my" herbicide (with the DuPont imprimatur) would be the key to success.

So in 1955 my little family was gathered up, wrenched from its placid security, and transported to Baltimore for the new adventure. We rented a big, more than adequate country house until we found a very nice new split-level—the fad of the time—to purchase. During the first year our third son, David, was born to the joy and excitement of all, with my mother visiting to help us.

My work involved writing promotional materials, calling on industrial and plant managers to sell them our custom weed-control services, acquiring equipment, and then actually doing the work with a few day-labor assistants. We bought a used fifteen-hundred-gallon oil delivery truck, cleaned it up, painted our logo on the side, and set forth. It had a long hose, extending several hundred feet to reach over fences into oil- and gasoline-tank storage farms.

We began with a few significant clients, but we quickly realized that contacting the vast number of companies, oil-tank farms, railroad lines and yards around Baltimore and up toward Philadelphia and New York, and securing them as clients would be an uphill struggle in the short run. Therefore a plan was developed for me to help out part-time with the company's established clients, to be their representative (and inspector) until my division came into profitability.

My associates felt that my personal attributes—a PhD, natural physical ability, outgoing personality, etc.—could easily be adapted to the work. One had to make inspections of all the operating facilities, find problems, and then report to the owners or managers. They could then make the proper control measures or let our company do the work. At first, this duty loomed as very dismal, considering my professional expertise and chosen career of plant science. But despite the expected loss in career experience, it turned out to be extremely interesting. My assigned clients—Doughnut Corporation of America, Scarlett's Seed Company, Luziane Coffee, Voneff Candy, and Guenther Brewing Company—had all sorts of fascinating operations that appealed to my curiosity, to say nothing of copious tasty samples inspectors were obliged to take. Sometimes I brought home sacks of flavored doughnuts for the family. There were enough commendations to assume that my way of carrying out my new responsibilities was quite agreeable to clients and my company supervisors as well.

I had come to this new work at about the same salary and benefits as before, with the expectation that rapid progress would justify rapid increases in remuneration. However, as time wore on it became obvious that the ongoing profit distribution was not going to benefit me in the foreseeable future. After a brief search I found a position as a horticulturist/plant physiologist in the USDA (US Department of Agriculture) in nearby Beltsville, Maryland.

I commuted twenty-five miles to work for about a year until we were sure this was the right move; it also took a while to find a suitable place to rent. The rental place was adequate if not great, and it was near schools for the boys, stores, and other amenities. Having already lived comfortably in two new houses, I resolved to build another, conveniently near my office, doing my own work at night and on weekends and sub-contracting some phases. We found a nice wooded lot half a mile from my work, purchased a prefabricated two-bedroom home similar to our first in Wilmington, and had it placed on a sufficiently raised, brick-veneered foundation to accommodate the kitchen/dining room, second bath and another bedroom, making it a full two-story house. With my designing, planning, landscaping, extensive carpentry, painting, etc., we effectively eliminated the need for an architect, general contractor, and construction supervisor, except for required city building-permit inspections. After living there almost eight years, we were handsomely rewarded for all this work in the price for which we sold it.

The USDA, based mostly in downtown Washington just south of the Mall, had installations all over the country. Agricultural research was based in Beltsville, a near suburb just east of the District of Columbia. It was there that Michael and Jeffrey were born.

Our home, located near the Plant Research headquarters, was close enough for me to walk to work, come home for lunch, and accommodate Ruth in our one-car situation. With my periodic trips all over the country to locations of my research work, her capabilities seemed unlimited and her attitude utterly cheerful as well. She was my mainstay, with supreme management of everything about home—shopping, schools for the boys, and constant assistance with children's programs in the Unitarian Fellowship we had joined.

A key subject for them was "The Church around the Corner," involving visits to and explanations of all major religions represented in the area. That exposure, which I shared, helped convince me of the unbelievable aspects of most religions. Whether or not my philosophy of Humanism/Naturalism has influenced my sons, I find it encouraging and significant that some fifty years later, none of them attends meetings of any widely known, publicly promoted religion. Hopefully they will find the majesty of all existence, temporal and cosmic, and satisfy the instinctive ultimate concern of humans in their own personal worlds; or they may, as I did somewhat belatedly, discover viable alternatives in such organized constructs as the Ethical Culture Society[27].

New Crops for the Country

Within the USDA and its Crops Research Division my work was in the New Crops Research Branch. At that time many of the major crops of the United States were in surplus production, and still the government struggled with troublesome crop subsidies. I came as a horticulturist/plant physiologist to the New Crops Research Branch, which was designed to find species with potential uses in the country, and to see if they could be grown successfully as crops. For many years before this, the USDA had sent botanists all over the world to find plants of interest to the U.S., either new or for improvement of existing crops. David Fairchild (*The World Was My Garden*) found and successfully introduced many palm species. Other plant explorers brought soybeans, safflower, castor beans, azaleas, and countless other ornamental species that were introduced from other parts of the world and later became established commercial crops. The plant-explorer botanists were then situated in the New Crops Research Branch, where agronomists, horticulturists, and other plant scientists were ready to conduct experiments to determine various plants' adaptability and utility in the United States.

An intermediate phase in the introduction of plants was performed in the four Utilization and Development Research Laboratories, where all sorts of evaluations were made, such as fiber content, chemical constituents, oil content, pharmaceutical properties, anti-cancer potential, etc.

My role was Investigations Leader for Chemurgic Crops, i.e. for chemical or

A farmer-contractor shows the author his field of *Crambe abyssinica*, Oregon

industrial uses such as fibers, oil seeds, pharmaceuticals, and insecticides. So I designed experiments to determine the climatic, soil, and cultivation requirements of promising selections from the Utilization Labs. We had federal experiment stations in Miami, Florida; Puerto Rico; Chico, California; Savannah, Georgia; and Ames, Iowa, and cooperative projects with many land-grant universities where plants could be grown experimentally. Among many prospect crops a few were singled out for research within limited budget restrictions.

Pharmaceutical

A few years before I began this research the "miracle drug" cortisone was found to have great promise for arthritis, inflammation treatment, and many other uses. As a steroidal compound its chemical relationship to testosterone and progesterone led to development of birth control drugs. Other plant species options for crop development could have been digitalis (an important drug for heart trouble derived from the foxglove plant), or reserpine (for hypertension, from Indian snakeroot—*Rauwolfia*); but the limited budget for all the good prospects simply demanded a choice based on current urgency of medical discoveries. Consequently we set forth on a program to domesticate several *Dioscorea* species as promising sources of steroidal precursors of cortisone. Margaret Kreig visited me in Beltsville and cited our work in her remarkably detailed scientific history of plants found to have valuable medicinal uses—*Green Medicine, The Search for Plants that Heal*. *Dioscorea alata*, also known as Mexican yam, is a chief plant-root source of food in tropical regions. Several species, *D. composita* and *D. spicuflora* (both poisonous, non-edible types used by natives for stunning or killing fish), were collected by our botanists, analyzed in the USDA labs, and found to contain variable amounts of diosgenin, which could be used to synthesize cortisone.

Our efforts were concentrated on methods for propagating plants collected principally in Guatemala and southern Mexico, where I made some exciting visits among the native inhabitants to see and study the local plant habitat. I designed and then directed greenhouse experiments (solution cultures) to determine optimal nutrient requirements (in Glendale, Maryland and Miami, Florida), propagating procedures, and field culture (in Los Angeles, Florida, and Puerto Rico). A primary rationale for our efforts was the prospect that the mushrooming effect of pharmaceutical demand for corticosteroids[28] would eradicate wild sources. However, additional sources might subsequently have been propagated in the wild or by agricultural production methods, including, possibly, some of those we developed; alternatively, laboratory efforts to synthesize them by other routes might have taken place.

OILSEEDS

Earlier milestones of the USDA were the introduction of soybeans and safflower, with their subsequent development into major American crops. Therefore, much effort in the utilization labs was directed toward other plants with useful oils for domestic and industrial purposes. The seed oil of *Crambe abyssinica* in the mustard family—related to rapeseed, already established as an oilseed crop—was found to have a very high percentage of erucic acid, useful in steel and plastics manufacturing.

As with all the initial studies of new crop possibilities, I contacted, negotiated with, and then distributed seed to cooperating state and federal experiment stations in various parts of the country, with proposed experiments to determine times of planting, spacing, depth of seeding, fertilization, and many other important aspects of cultivation. As our work with *Crambe* progressed, along with three or more others simultaneously, the possibility came to me that we could do some intensive study of the actual growth and development of each species, to delineate their geographic climatic requirements by simply analyzing their daily growth responses to the incredibly complicated array of physical (i.e., weather-related) conditions that happen everywhere daily.

My thoughts were enhanced by the current research of my former graduate school acquaintance Joseph Higgins, with whom we had social contacts. His first position with the Seabrook Frozen Food Company in New Jersey, working for his father-in-law, the noted climatologist C. W. Thornthwaite[29], involved the study of plant development relative to environmental variations caused by multitudes of seasonal weather conditions. The company needed to schedule plantings of each crop (e.g. peas) so as to provide predictable, relatively uniform harvest supplies for their processing operations. Thornthwaite suggested that Higgins make daily counts of the number of leaves on a representative sample of marked plants so that their average development from day to day could possibly be correlated with actual weather variables. If so, they could subsequently make planting schedules based on the progress of weather conditions each season, and thus prevent, or at least dampen, the uneven supply of the crop for processing—a task they successfully accomplished.

With this background experience, Higgins subsequently accepted our offer of a position in the New Crops Branch to do studies with our new-crop prospects to help find ideal climatic locations throughout the country. That is, the ability to explicitly characterize the most desirable seasonal weather and environmental conditions at just one or several locations would shortcut the expense of multiple trials all over the country.

The results of this landmark research were published in 1964[30] with studies of *Crambe*[31], *Hibiscus cannabinus* (kenaf)[32], *Tephrosia*[33], and corn (as a contrast to the relatively unknown new species).

Fiber Crops for Paper

In the area of fiber crops for paper pulp we were considering annual sources such as *Crotalaria*, hemp, and kenaf, and a perennial source, bamboo. I was responsible for the experimental work (principally bamboo) at the Savannah station, involving distribution of propagating material for ornamental purposes and experimentation.

For annual sources we chose for experimental trials the tall large-stemmed species of *Crotalaria, Hibiscus* (kenaf) and *Cannabis* (hemp). For many decades, perhaps one could say since the beginnings of our country, hemp was the chief source of cordage fiber, which in turn was essential for rope on naval ships. Consequently our government had the foresight to stockpile sufficient seed sources to initiate domestic production in case we were cut off from the mostly foreign sources of cordage during

Joseph Higgins records daily growth of kenaf (*Hibiscus cannabinus*)

any war-time embargoes. One of our responsibilities (aptly related to all non-established crops) was to sustain storage of large quantities of hemp seed in several Midwestern seed storage facilities, i.e. making periodic checks of germination viability and replenishing if necessary. However, a few years before World War II, the advent of synthetic fibers (nylon, etc.) gradually resulted in obsolescence of "natural" fibers, although we still held the stored seed.

An amusing incident occurred in our work on these experiments. Neither I, nor my immediate supervision, was aware at the time (late 1950s) of the growing concern for the use of marijuana as obtained from hemp, so we embarked on experimental plantings, along with *Crotalaria* and kenaf. A progressive farmer, closely attuned to the research of his nearest university experiment station, contacted me to see if he could obtain enough hemp seed for a small planting—perhaps half an acre—so as to have early knowledge of production in the event successful commercial production was undertaken. We saw this as a nice free gesture that might even help with our program, so I ordered out a twenty-pound shipment to him in Oshkosh, Wisconsin. About ten days later word came down from "upper management" that this was currently a no-no. There must have been some other government agency—a predecessor to today's Drug Enforcement Agency—with considerable concern about hemp seed shipments. I was confronted with:

"Joe, did you send twenty pounds of hemp seed to…."

"Yes."

"You think you could get it back?"

"Well, I don't know, but the farmer sounded quite friendly on the phone. If he hasn't planted it yet I guess he might let us have it back for some friendly reason. How quick do you want it?"

"Today!"

It was fairly early in the morning, so I got the farmer on the phone, and possibly out of bed.

"Have you planted the seed yet?

"No."

"Sorry to trouble you with our plans but we have decided it would be best not to make plantings other than on our experiment stations just now and wondered if we could get the seed back."

"Oh, sure, that'll be okay with me."

"If it's okay, I'll be there later today."

I jumped in my car, drove to the National Airport, luckily caught the next plane to Chicago with a good connection for Oshkosh, rented a car, found his farm and brought the seed back to Beltsville. Needless to say, we quickly removed hemp from our experiments.

Kenaf was found to be superior to *Crotalaria*, and we demonstrated successful production in several parts of the country. That is, tonnage of dry material per acre per year equaled or surpassed that of pine trees as used for paper pulp. As with all newly discovered sources of raw materials there is a considerable time lag before existing industries become interested, then do all the research and engineering of pilot plants and, finally, launch a "new crop." Contacts with potential firms, offers of free pilot quantities of fiber, and possibly other inducements, are essential.

Bamboo was an entirely different fiber source, since it could be considered only as a perennial crop rather than an annual. Botanically bamboo is unique, as it is the largest grass and among the fastest-growing plants in the world. There are two main types, tropical and temperate. Since the portion of the United States where tropical types will grow is much smaller than areas suitable for temperate species, our efforts were concentrated in the Southern states.

During this period we contracted with the Herty Foundation, a nonprofit research and development organization with expertise in pulp and paper research for the paper industry, to make experimental quantities of paper using several species of bamboo. It had been recognized that there had been extensive use of bamboo for paper in the Orient and India, so there was the question of the suitability of our domestically grown bamboo for paper pulp.

Bamboo varieties growing in Richmond Hill, GA experimental plots

A summary of this work was published in *Fiber and Papermaking Characteristics of Bamboo,* Technical Bulletin No 1361, in 1966. A few quotations from this publication may be of interest:

As a rule, bamboo fibers are about the same length as those of hardwood but are shorter than those of most coniferous woods, and have higher length-to-width ratios than conifers. High length-to-width ratios indicate that bamboo fibers are flexible and strong rather than stiff and brittle. Slender, pliable fibers are better for most paper because they give softness and smoothness rather than hardness and coarseness to the product. These characteristics indicate that bamboo may have use in the manufacture of high-quality material for facial tissue and for book, bond, and stationery products.

Bamboo can be pulped readily with less power and chemicals than wood. We plunged into several experiments to determine methods for planting, cultivating, fertilizing, harvesting, and storing it. One was with a tropical species at Belle Glade, Florida; two with temperate species were undertaken in South Carolina and Alabama.

Each of the experiments with temperate species needed one hundred acres of land, in order to have sufficient plot size, even though we were trying to answer only the most elementary questions: Which species would be best? What level of fertilization would be best? What system of harvest would be best? Of course, you can imagine the need for space between plots was critical because of the running nature of temperate species.

The cost to sustain such a program over the long period that would be necessary—perhaps ten to twenty years—would be considerable. Therefore, cooperative agreements for financing the experiments were negotiated between the land-grant universities and the USDA. The total outlay for the agronomic development of bamboo for paper pulp in the United States was estimated as $35,000 to $50,000 per year—which translated to a total of $350,000 to $1,000,000 (for the ten- to twenty-year period) to answer the original questions. In addition, there would have been a considerable expense to develop a pilot plant for the pulping and/or inducement of private enterprise to do so.

Several paper companies were quite interested in our activities, but never to the extent of carrying out agronomic research, or participating in the over-all program. Although these costs, by today's standards, were relatively low, it was evident that state university budgets alone would not be sufficient to establish any totally new crop—whether bamboo or any other—without the support of a nationally funded program. This unfortunate situation was probably impacted by the fact that "new crops" had no lobbying capacity comparable to those already in place for existing commercial crops (corn, wheat, soybeans etc.) and their related industries.

As a result, the efforts toward crop development for bamboo gradually waned. Yet according to Maureen Smith's *The U.S. Paper Industry and Sustainable Production*, our per-capita paper consumption in the United States is now over seven hundred pounds per year, by far the highest in the world. Furthermore, global production in the pulp, paper, and publishing sector in 2020 is expected to increase by 77 percent from 1995 levels (OECD Environmental Outlook, 2001, p.215). The southern United States is presently the largest paper-producing region in the world (USDA Forest Service Southern Forest Research Assessment, 2001). It is estimated that, because of its sustainable growth habits, bamboo would produce several times more cellulose per acre per year than conventional forest products.

In *The U.S. Paper Industry and Sustainable Production* Maureen Smith writes:

> The best research that has been done on nonwood pulping has been done by the U. S. Department of Agriculture. A wonderful research project that began in the 1950s and was ongoing through the 1960s resulted in a series of technical research papers evaluating the use of agricultural materials to make pulp from a whole range of different angles: how to pulp them, how to process them, how to recover them, the economics, the expectations for farmers. It was a very comprehensive body of research, but it resulted in nothing. We have never really backed up the potential that we know is there. We're waiting for industry, I suppose, to pick up on it. But given the way the paper industry is organized—very intensive integration with the forest and forest products industries as a whole—it is naïve to think that the industry is going to run with a completely different alternative source of fiber. But the potential has been documented.

The author's wife Ruth with their five sons in Beltsville: L-R: Mike, Alan, Jeff, David, Steve

Chapter 7

Savannah-Richmond Hill Interlude

The second of two great enigmas in my life came at Beltsville. It was an ill-fated attempt to bring into reality the hope of using bamboo for paper pulp. While in the USDA I had encouraged the people who were considering commercial development of this project, and I was subsequently enticed, by a very generous salary, to join them in this effort. Again I wrenched my "little" family, now comprising five sons and Ruth's mother, from a secure and comfortable situation to another, with hopefully desirable living conditions, despite the subtropical climate. Of course, all moving expenses were paid.

It began with an idea in the Monsanto chemical company. They had developed and patented a method for pulping paper with a nitrate (or nitrite) basis instead of the conventional sulfite methods, which are associated with the offensive sulfur-dioxide odors near many pulp mills. However, nitrate methods would be much more expensive. The idea evolved that recycling the nitrogen-rich effluent from the mills could be a practical way to provide fertilization for the crop (bamboo) and help achieve economic viability.

After much consideration the company decided that the forecasted potential profit margin was not sufficient to proceed with the project. Several upper-level company executives who had been so interested and engaged in the research decided they would put their money together and try to do it independently of Monsanto. Somehow, they arranged with the company to let them use their process patent under a license or royalty basis. They had to choose a location with available farmland, water, suitable climate, and favorable conditions for construction of a mill.

They selected the former Ford Plantation at the little town of Richmond Hill, south of Savannah, Georgia. They knew that it would take quite a number of years to acquire enough additional land on which to propagate and grow bamboo to a size sufficient for harvest—to say nothing of the time to raise money for construction of a mill. Therefore they decided to utilize the land during the developmental period to grow commercial vegetable crops that would provide some cash-flow until production could begin.

I was a party to these ideas, but from the outset it was understood that, while I was a professional horticulturist, my principal role would be to secure bamboo-propagating material, and grow and harvest it in vast quantities for the mill. They would obtain information from the state university and supervision for the production of vegetable crops.

It took only one season—fifty acres of potatoes later—to discover that the production of vegetables on untested soil, with no established labor or marketing procedures in the area, would not work in the short run, and probably not in the long run. Of course, I had no idea of how much money they started with, or could reasonably secure in the future. I did know it would ultimately take millions of dollars and many more years.

For whatever their final considerations, the project came to an abrupt end. I then came to Clemson University to do research on various crops and to develop methods for quantifying daily plant growth in response to environmental conditions.

New Crop Triumphs

As with most basic research, commercial success was not reached quickly. Without detailing all imaginable thoughts and program strategies for domestication of wild plants, it is of interest to recall some other candidate species that were proposed: spice bush, *Lindera benzoin* for lauric acid; Stokes aster (*Stokesia sp.*) for epoxy fatty acid; *Lesquerella sp.* for hydroxyl acids; jojoba for long-chain fatty acids; *Pyrethrum* and *Tephrosia* for insecticides; foxglove (*Digitalis*) for digitalin; and snakeroot, (*Rauwolfia sp.*) for reserpine. We had test plots of these and many other plants at different sites throughout the country, but because of budgetary limitations could expand to developmental experiments with only a few. We tested for outstanding chemical and/or physical properties in combination with vigorous health and success at growing. When I left the USDA none of the species with which I had worked were considered successful commercially. The modest requests for research budget increases from year to year were invariably reduced, and the total outlay for the entire U.S. was around seven-and-a-half annual man-years of effort (including myself and fractions of persons in regional USDA locations and cooperating states' experiment stations). The lack of a public advocacy group, or "lobbying potential," for new crops comparable to that for major crop and animal industries was surely a factor.

Despite the many years of eager, hopeful planning of experimental work with many successful results, it was somewhat depressing that no significant start or development of a new crop for the country—like soybeans many years before—could be realized.

Now, as this is being written about fifty years later, it is incredibly satisfying to find that success has actually been attained with *Crambe* and kenaf. Albeit relatively few thousands of acres are involved, the fact that successful farm production and appropriate industrial adaptations have been made in several states gives me a great sense of accomplishment after all.

THE CLEMSON YEARS—STUDYING ENVIRONMENTAL FACTORS IN PLANT GROWTH

Our decision to move to Clemson University, instead of accepting an offer to return to the USDA, was based on friendships and experimental cooperation stretching back through each of my previous professional positions. It also grew out of my hope for expanding my methodology for relating daily development of plants to weather variables in such a way as to make early crop-yield predictions during the growing season. Knowing this might have immediate commercial and scientific potential, through contacts and inquiries from industrial firms in my previous jobs, I was given a position, based on my confident promise that I could find research grant funds for such a program. Over the next few years I was able to secure over $250,000 in various contracts from NASA and other government agencies. This not only justified my salary, but gave me a degree of freedom to employ help, buy equipment, and travel. I also benefited from the fact that I could accept consulting arrangements, generally not a possibility for federal employees.

My professional employment had included both government and private industry (a major corporation and two small companies), and now I was in the final and most desirable position for creativity and freedom of action—the university. I designed a course for graduate students, Quantitative Morphology, to embody the methodology that we developed in the USDA to quantify daily development of plants using a unique index that could be used to correlate variable daily values of weather and other environmental factors. Some of the graduate students taking my course chose, with my encouragement, to make an intense study of single crop species in preparation for writing their masters theses. To fuel this work, as well as pursue my own research goals without burdening limited departmental funds, I wrote proposals for appropriate research projects to submit to government agencies and interested industries. This required an element of salesmanship as well as some interesting travel to visit and confer with prospective sponsors.

Though there was no particular publicity at that time recognizing what I consider the prime achievement of my professional career, my development of the *Haun scale*[34] for quantifying plant development (with potential use in predicting crop yields), my published papers and talks doubtless resulted in most of my consulting arrangements.

A consulting project with the Coca-Cola Company resulted from work we had done in the USDA. One of the presumed critical elements of their signature product was obtained from a plant species growing in a province in China that had become impossible to obtain because of the political situation of the time. The company possessed some small plants of this species in the Florida greenhouses of its subsidiary Minute Maid® and wanted us to see if we could develop ways to propagate and establish production somewhere in the United States or other cooperative locations. From this initial project their interest broadened to an interest in my designing an experimental plan to adapt my methodology to citrus crops, principally oranges. Yields were notably uneven from year to year with questionable, or at best vague, explanations relating to daily weather and environmental variables. My recommendations for data collection by their technicians enabled me to develop equations for input of weather variables that would provide timely predictions of probable yields at the end of the season. This information, of course, was useful in subsequent plans for irrigation timing or other cultivation practices, but probably more important for predicting harvesting and sales outcomes.

I consulted with other companies with similar objectives, including potato production by a large producer of dehydrated potato flakes in England, banana production in Honduras, and production of grain, wheat, oats, barley, corn, etc. for companies trading these commodities.

Family

The twenty years at Clemson embrace wonderful memories as they encompassed fulfillment of our lives embodied in the development of our five sons. While I was engrossed in professional duties, Ruth undertook Herculean achievements, arranging for schools from preschool through high school as well as numerous extracurricular activities. In addition, she organized the first church school for the Unitarian fellowship in which we were charter members, started a League of Women Voters chapter, handled shopping and house work, and still managed to do some very interesting art work.

To begin this venture we needed a new house—a big one. As before, we took a one-year lease on a four-bedroom place for all the boys and Grandma Smith, Ruth's mother. Then plans were laid for a new place, to be built on weekends, nights, and vacation, paid for with the profits made on sales of earlier homes. Since Clemson is located on a large lake with potential views of the mountains from high points, I resolved to find a site combining these features. About two miles north of town we found such a place in a new section of residential property. Since it was outside the city water-distribution area, our purchase was contingent on securing water from a well to be drilled at our expense.

With Ruth's suggestions I quickly made a pencil set of plans for a forty-five-hundred-square-foot house: three floors contained four-and-a-half baths, five bedrooms with study on the second floor, a large living/dining space, storage, and bedroom on the first floor, and two fireplaces. Thus, Grandma and all the boys (except the youngest, Jeff and Mike, who shared) would have their own rooms. I took the plans to a Clemson architectural student who needed extra income and who converted them to engineering blueprints. This simple step saved untold amounts in architect and developer fees. With the understanding that I, acting as the "builder," would arrange for labor and subcontracts, the local bank gave us a construction loan.

One fine spring day, we borrowed a surveyor's level and Alan and I placed the "batter boards" to establish corners of the house on the property. Batter boards are well outside the actual corners in order to stretch strings at the precise positions of the outside dimensions and their elevations. Thus, the strings can be removed for various operations, then reattached, and remain in place until ditches for footings are dug, foundation poured, and walls started. A backhoe operator was hired to dig the partially above-ground basement and footing space.

Meanwhile, a well-driller was engaged, and we picked a spot about seventy-five feet from the house for him to start. After several days' drilling, to a depth exceeding three hundred feet, he had, sadly, found no water. Drilling cost about five dollars per foot (cheap by present-day values) but was an immediate concern since the next step was to pick another site and try again. This was done with the earlier proviso by the seller of the land, that if we could not find water on our lot we could go elsewhere on the total properties and drill. With this unhappy prospect I suddenly remembered the explanation by my brother, then advising locations for oil and gas wells in the Rocky Mountain area, of how dynamiting had been used to fracture subterranean formations and possibly induce production. I asked the driller if he had ever tried it. He said he had, but with no success and furthermore that it was a bit dangerous.

Since he was unwilling to try it, I asked if he would mind if I tried "before he moved the drilling rig to the next location." He agreed and left for the day. It was about noon so I discussed my plan with my backhoe operator; he, having some experience in dynamiting for highway construction, agreed to help.

He advised me, "Go to a hardware store up at Pickens and buy half a case of dynamite sticks, several caps—be sure not to carry them near the case of dynamite—a roll of two-strand electrical extension wire, a four-foot piece of plastic pipe, and a roll of stout nylon twine." Caps, the small thumbnail-sized items with two wires extending for electrical connections, are very dangerous to handle, and must be stored separately from the dynamite.

I was back in several hours and we set about to prepare a device to lower into the six-inch drilled hole. The driller had mentioned that at a depth of about one hundred-seventy-five feet the bit had stuck briefly, indicating a possible fracture in the solid stone being penetrated. Thinking this would be a good depth to set it off, we measured this length of electrical cord and twine to attach to the device, which was constructed by sliding bundles of dynamite sticks into the plastic pipe, carefully placing a blasting cap, with wires attached, about the middle. Then we began to lower it into the hole, taking turns as it was quite heavy. Suddenly, before we reached the desired depth, the cord and wire snapped and, with an audible swish and splash, went to the bottom in the residual pool of drilling water (used for lubricating the bit).

What to do? It was late in the day, the sun about to go down, and the driller was coming back in the morning. We decided to try to activate the explosion by putting another cap down on top of the device at the bottom of the well. Three-hundred-plus feet of wire and cord were again measured and attached to a brick (for weight) and again lowered carefully until a faint splash indicated it was near the device.

During our operations the sun had gone down, but fortunately we could continue with a full moon. The ultimate moment arrived. We took the excess wire from the cap in the well over to his truck, about one hundred feet away, lifted the hood and touched the wires to the battery—THUD!—we felt a slight ground tremor, then WHOOCH!—and a huge geyser of water shot into the moonlit sky above the trees. After it fell we ran over to the wellhead and listened—WATER RUNNING! Our spirits soared, but the sound wasn't sustained, it was only the drill water draining back to the bottom. The next day the driller tested for any success and found none, at which time he moved the rig to another, lower point several hundred feet away.

We theorized later about what we could have done differently. The most obvious possibility was that we should have packed the well with sand above the dynamite to concentrate the explosive force in the ground as opposed to up the well shaft. We also realized we were lucky the upward force had not loosened the heavy twenty-foot steel well-casing at the top and sent it up in the air, then down on us. Anyway, there was enough time, money and emotional exertion spent in the project to keep us from trying it again.

Sadly, the second site also proved to be a dry hole. I had phoned some sources of information and found that government contractors would drill only to two hundred-fifty feet, then stop if no water was found, so this is where we stopped. Then we moved down the hill about a thousand feet, still on the development property, and found water at a depth of one hundred-fifty feet. The uncomfortable total cost, including underground piping to the house, was somewhat moderated by the prospect of selling water to a neighbor for several years until city water reached us. Luckily, there were no more setbacks, and the house was "finished" enough for us to move in that fall.

Though tedious at times, the joys of family life were great for a long period. Ruth wove me into action at PTA meetings, Boy Scout trips, and many social activities. Since the boys had various acquaintances with whom they participated in group trips, I tried to go with each one on individual camping, shopping, or sports event trips. Perhaps we would pack food and gear for overnight, take our canoe and paddle up the lake to its upper reaches, find a little island, make camp, and build a fire for supper in front of our tent—feeling like Tom Sawyer and Huckleberry Finn. Other trips were up the mountains to other isolated sites with our favorite dog, Augie.

University professors were given priority for tickets to sports events, so the whole family had some very good fifty-yard seats at football games and close-in basketball seats as well. My preferred sports were tennis and racquetball. All the boys were involved in one or more school sports, community soccer, and baseball, so Ruth's car-pooling was constant.

Our cornucopian family travels were cherished memories: in one thirteen-month period we covered twenty thousand miles, including Nova Scotia, the Everglades, and the Pacific Northwest. I always had a yen for travel, but never enough money to do it, yet somehow I managed—starting in college with hitchhiking over ten thousand miles. At first, with seven in the family, our transportation was a nine-passenger station wagon with luggage rack on top. Naturally, camping in state and federal parks or forest campgrounds was the normal venue. We loved the out-of-doors, cooking over fires and sleeping in tents, and everyone participated gleefully in the duties. My limited vacation time was frequently augmented by combining family trips with professional visits to universities or experiment stations that were cooperating in my research projects.

As the family grew we soon added a small two-wheeled utility trailer, then graduated to a fold-out camper trailer. Four slept in the trailer, two in the station wagon, and one in a pup tent. We not only carried all the usual essential gear, but also a huge tarpaulin to cover all operations in case of rain. We would attach a rope ten or more feet high between two trees, far enough apart to cover our picnic table, and have the grill or fire at one end. After we were set up, weather was rarely a problem. Except on one occasion, evidencing our determination to avoid motel stays, we arrived in late afternoon at a lovely campsite in a coastal Maine location. It had been pouring rain for hours, with no sign of lessening. With the family in the station wagon reading and listening to music, I put on rain gear (pants and coat), climbed two trees, stretched the rope, spread the tarpaulin and tied it to other trees. Then I set forth to find, and sometimes chop up, firewood. Defying old Boy Scout traditions, with a little paper and kerosene I had a rousing fire going in about thirty minutes. Soon we had the water boiling for clams acquired earlier, a great meal, and cheer before sleeping-bag time. No matter where we were—at home or on trips—we always held hands, eyes closed, for a moment of silence before meals.

Though our North American travels were extensive, the boys had wonderful first tastes of European adventure. Ruth's parents had emigrated from England after World War I and had made periodic return visits. Grandma Smith, now living with us, wanted the boys to see where they had lived and meet some of their relatives, and she subsidized our fares so that we could accompany her. Ruth's cousin, John Smith, lent us a car in England. By visiting relatives and staying at many bed-and-breakfast places, we covered the country from Devon and Cornwall to East Anglia. Compared with today, prices were not outrageous in those days: sometimes the whole family could stay in a B&B for twenty-five dollars.

Many were the inspirations Ruth and I experienced from visiting the homes of famous literary figures and awesome cathedrals begun in medieval times. Especially poignant to us were the homes of Wordsworth and Sir Walter Scott, my boyhood favorite, in the Lake District. I imagined, when looking at Scott's study desk, that it might have been the place he sat when writing *Ivanhoe* or *Quentin*

Durward. Of approximately forty major cathedrals and minsters, we visited over twenty in the years of our trips. Unlike many tourists taking extended commercial tours who "can't stand to see another *church*," I was intrigued by every one. All are different, artistic, truly monuments, almost unbelievable structural examples of creativity, in days far before the advent of electricity, machine tools, and pneumatic devices—and all, of course, built on the backs of the poor.

My sense of wonder would also apply to many other cathedrals visited in later years in Germany, France, and Italy, as well as Islamic mosques in Turkey. Philosophically, I took away the inevitable impression that the driving force behind their construction must have been fanatic devotion or faith in imaginary religious beliefs, as opposed to utilitarian constructions. We cannot know to what extent that devotion was shared by the laborers, or how many of them worked under duress. On the other hand, if it can be said that these structures have supplied continuous, essential symbols of inspiration needed to sustain life, then perhaps we should build more of them. However, current sober judgment relative to religious fanaticism and the need for more practical structures would suggest that they be relegated to the museum of beautiful anthropological and archaeological curiosities.

After the boys were launched in college they, too, had formative travel experiences: David and Michael on study trips to Europe, Steve to India, Jeffrey to England and Norway during my sabbatical there, and Alan to the South Pacific on many trips for his PhD research.

In addition to the joy of travel with the boys, touring opportunities expanded for Ruth and me as well. My professional meetings and consulting ventures reached Mexico, Honduras, Guatemala, England, Switzerland, and Germany. Trips were replete with chances to visit outstanding or historic places. About 1975, in connection with one of my research projects, financed by grant funds, I wanted to obtain plant-growth observation data in a wide variety of environmental situations. In order to extend the universe of data beyond typical production areas in the U.S., I arranged to have data collected in England, Norway, and Germany.

At this time the Haun scale had not been recognized widely in plant science literature. This was in part because it was developed on little-known potential "new" crops and only in a limited way on established crops, and actually recognized as a useful tool only in our work with wheat. The project in Europe involved corn,

Zea mays as we know it (in Europe wheat is usually thought of as corn), and the subjective visual scale for recording growth incrementals had to be adapted to corn.

We wanted data on a daily basis for an entire season. Thus, after beginning correspondence with each location, it was necessary for me to visit and give a hands-on explanation for plant observations and the data desired. Locations were with government research stations at Long Ashton (Bristol), England; Ås, Norway; and Munich, Germany. After test plots were planted and plants had developed a few leaves, a three-week trip was scheduled. I supplemented the budgeted expense involved and utilized a few days of annual leave so that Ruth could accompany me. For economy and convenience we used Eurail transportation. Unlike government, the university did not frown upon my use of supplemental personal funds and leave. It was a grand, enjoyable, totally successful trip. Of course, we visited a few relatives in England and some classic historic places in Germany and Norway.

A Sudden Loss

A sad postscript of the trip was a problem, seemingly of acute indigestion, that Ruth experienced a few times. Months before the trip she had visited our family doctor and a specialist in internal medicine as well, and was told there was no serious condition to prohibit such a trip. This incorrect diagnosis had a tragic result for Ruth and her family when, after the trip, it was discovered that she had cancer. My letter to friends and family explained in more detail.

> Clemson, South Carolina
> May 1, 1978
>
> We are very sorry to send the sad news that Ruth's long battle with cancer is over. Please excuse this photocopied letter, but we thought you would want the news before any more time elapsed. So many people in and around Clemson have been of assistance to Ruth and to the family that we still have not been able to acknowledge all of the thoughtful things they have done.
>
> Two and a half years ago, just after our trip to Europe, it was discovered that Ruth had some form of cancer. A

major operation confirmed this discovery and indicated that the situation was very serious. We took her to the M. D. Anderson Hospital at the Texas Medical Center in Houston, Texas, for three weeks of observation and tests. They diagnosed it as Diffuse Histiocytic Lymphoma and recommended high-level chemotherapy in the Laminar Flow Protected Environment for two months or more. At first this solitary confinement, including Christmas in the hospital, seemed like an unbearably lonely type of treatment, but Ruth was very courageous and came through with flying colors. She was considered as a very good patient and the cancer was in remission. After returning home she was put on a maintenance treatment of chemotherapy at 3-4 week intervals. Each of these made her quite ill for a day or so, but in between treatments she felt normal and was able to enjoy life very well for about eighteen months. In fact, she later said that it had been one of the happiest periods of her life. We did many things we had always wanted to, and enjoyed many accomplishments of the boys, and their activities.

Then, last fall, further development of the problem was evident and another major operation confirmed the spread of tumors. We were most discouraged. But, again, there was hope in a new type of even more intensive chemotherapy, involving removal of bone marrow for later rejuvenation of the blood manufacturing system after the treatment. This would also require the transfer of leucocytes from all of the boys if possible. Ruth was not eager for this plan, after the operation and the great disappointment of the findings. Therefore, several other more conventional chemotherapy drugs were tried. The situation became worse and she finally decided to go through with the high-level treatment and bone marrow rescue on January 1. Although successful, the treatment was a very harrowing experience. She probably received a record number of supplementary treatments and new processes during the two-month period. Three of the boys gave leucocytes daily for three or four days each. Her recovery was slow but considered remarkably good by the many doctors involved. At last she come home and was so happy to be here. She was due to go back in two weeks to Houston for establishment of a maintenance level of chemotherapy, but, to our dismay, pain began to occur in different places than before, only a week after she was home. We quickly returned to Houston where her situation became worse. Her suffering was kept to a minimum with medication and she died peacefully on March 27.

After such a successful and happy life with Ruth it is hard to endure the thought of her absence. We are gradually trying to put our lives back together. The boys are a great comfort and help to me. Ruth's life was a wonderful example to them and an inspiration to live useful lives of service to others.

Many of our friends participated in a memorial service for Ruth, some reading favorite poetry and others speaking about Ruth's life. I include a sampling of what Ruth's memory meant to some of those friends.

Remember

Remember me when I am gone away,
    Gone far away into the silent land;
When you can no more hold me by the hand,
    Nor I half turn to go, yet turning stay.
Remember me when no more, day by day,
    You tell me of our future that you planned:
Only remember me; you understand
    It will be late to counsel then or pray.

Yet if you should forget me for a while
    And afterwards remember, do not grieve:

For if the darkness and corruption leave
    A vestige of the thoughts that once I had,
Better by far you should forget and smile
    Than that you should remember and be sad.

Christina Georgina Rosetti (1830-1894)

A Song of Living

Because I have loved life, I shall have no sorrow to die.
I have sent up my gladness on wings,
    to be lost in the blue of the sky.
I have run and leaped with the rain,
    I have taken the wind to my breast.
My cheek like a drowsy child to the face of the earth I have pressed.

Because I have loved life, I shall have no sorrow to die.
I have kissed young Love on the lips,
    I have heard his song to the end.
I have struck my hand like a seal
    in the loyal hand of a friend.
I have known the peace of heaven,
    the comfort of work done well.
I have longed for death in the darkness and risen alive out of hell.

Because I have loved life, I shall have no sorrow to die.
I give a share of my soul
    to the world where my course is run.
I know that another shall finish
    the task I must leave undone.
I know that no flower, no flint
    was in vain on the path I trod.
As one looks on a face through a window,
    through life I have looked on God.
Because I have loved life, I shall have no sorrow to die.

Amelia Josephine Burr (1878-1968)

Memories from Sharon Fennell

Ruth Haun served as president of the provisional League of Women Voters of the Clemson Area from 1968 to 1970. She later served as chairman of the Education and Human Resources portfolios and as state Child Welfare chair, leading studies in curriculum, foster care and family courts. The League and Ruth believe that democratic government depends upon the informed and active participation of its citizens…[and] that responsible government should be responsive to the will of the people. As President, Ruth wrote many messages to the members. I would like to share a few with you.

In her first message Ruth thanked the Preliminary Committee. She said, "Their initial enthusiasm and hard work are responsible for our existence as a League. In League study and discussion I feel we will all gain a feeling of personal satisfaction from becoming more informed as citizens and voters, and through League Action and Voter Service we can hope to make a positive contribution to our community, state, and nation."

It is not an easy thing to form a new League. There are positions to review, reports to fill out, surveys to be written and community leaders to be contacted. The paperwork seemed endless. One message recalls, "My son said to me as he surveyed a stack of mail from state and national offices, 'If you want to DO something, why don't you just go out and do it and not bother with all this?'" Others have said, "Well, I'm really upset about—so I'm thinking about joining the League." To the first question I talk about strength in numbers, and to the other I say, "Great! We need you. But don't expect miracles." Later she wrote about the importance of members in forming a new League. "How much our League can do to provide a variety of services to voters will depend upon your enthusiastic response. This is our chance to demonstrate to the community that the League does make a difference."

At the time of Martin Luther King's death the League of Women Voters of the United States issued a statement, accompanied by a letter from the national president. The statement and letter were to reach each member. Ruth wrote, "Knowing that not everyone will take the same view, I have debated whether or not to include them in our bulletin. However, it would be wrong to quietly tuck them away in the files. Solutions to problems are not found by hiding from the problems. And we all know that solutions to the problems our country is faced with must be found. In the comfort of our homes and in the beauty of spring in Clemson these problems seem far away and not quite real. But they are real and they are not far away, if we will only choose to see them."

The author's grandparents, his father Charles (left) and uncle Ray (right)

Vanderbilt University School of Religion Faculty 1927-28. Prof. Charles C. Haun is third row, second from left

The author's father, Charles C. Haun, as an Army chaplain in 1918 (left, above) and as a new graduate in 1921 (left, below).

The Cumberland Homestead house, Crossville, TN, in which the author spent part of his childhood

In the early years of the twentieth century, rural life in the southern Appalachians was virtually unchanged from the 1800s. Stone and wooden houses were built using local materials, while planting and harvesting relied on the labor of farm animals and human labor. Within the author's lifespan, mechanized equipment replaceed horses, mules, and oxen, and a system of production and distribution that has come to be known as "agribusiness" replaced traditional farm life.

A horse-drawn binder used for wheat, oats, and barley on the Haun family farm, ca.1916

The barn at the Cumberland homestead

The author's father riding the hay wagon after a harvest

Grandpa and Grandma Smith with Ruth, Steven, and Alan

Jeff, Alan, and Mike with their mother, on a camping trip in the Florida Everglades

The boys at Savannah Beach, 1964

Family—past, present, and future—has been a central part of the author's life. From learning about, and from, his forebears to watching his five sons grow to adulthood and find their own places in the world, the author has observed and contemplated his own and their lives. When the boys were young he took them and their mother on camping trips around the United States, and as they grew older they went on European visits for enlightenment, education, business, and pleasure.

Betsy, a beloved member of the Haun family

Mike and Jeff visit Stonehenge

Jeff compares the grandeur of Salisbury Cathedral with the ruins of Tintern Abbey

Steve with pet himalayan rabbits at home in Beltsville, MD

David in costume for a family theatrical, Swannanoa, NC

Each of the author's five sons learned to follow his own path in life. Alan went to Columbia, S.C., then Eugene, Oregon, and finally to the South Pacific where he is a professional in both anthropology and archaeology. Steve moved to Swannanoa, N.C. to study horticulture at Warren Wilson College and became a landscape architect. David chose to work as a city and regional planner in government service. Michael attended Penn State for graduate study as a ceramics engineer. After college in Atlanta and Eugene, OR, Jeff opted for public outreach through media production.

Jeff holding a bowl of raspberries at Ingonish Beach, Nova Scotia

Mike in a field of broadbeans, East Anglia

Alan in the Everglades

The little mermaid, sculpted in honor of Hans Christian Anderson, guards the harbor in Copenhagen, Denmark

A zoo filled with exotic African animals in rural England

Vigeland Sculpture Park, Oslo, Norway

One of the author's favorite formal English gardens

The author with Helen In Tangier, Morocco

Toledo, Spain, known from the 8th to 15th centuries for its cosmopolitanism and tolerance, a unique city where Jews, Christians, and Muslims coexisted peacefully.

Helen, Lucas, and the author create a Christmas image

The author with President and Mrs. Carter, 2002

David with President Reagan, ca. 1984

The author with writer Richard Dawkins at the 70th Anniversary Conference of the American Humanist Association, Boston, 2011

Chapter 8

A New Start

At this point in my life I was devastated—sometimes unable to find a way to take the next breath. I paced around the yard thinking of all the places we had been in our lives, things we had enjoyed together, how Ruth looked and what she said. I had been so optimistic, confident that somehow there would be a miraculous recovery—but now it was over. I would have been overwhelmed by grief if not for the boys' comfort and reassurance.

Responsibilities of my work plus diversions of travel gradually bridged the huge vacuum that was created and, to a great extent, continued. My life had proceeded at such an intense pace, without time for reflection or appreciation of all its meanings. Ruth's prodigious accomplishments with the family and community, and our realization that her philosophy of religion and meaning of life were identical with mine, have forever been mainstays to me.

Several people in the community, knowing of my dejected state, invited me to meet and try to become acquainted with some new people, and other acquaintances suggested that I join a group called Parents without Partners. At first I was reluctant and asked David if he thought it proper for me to do. With his assent I joined, and subsequently I met Helen, who became my unconditional companion.

Meanwhile, my sister Margaret and her family invited Jeff and me to join them for a backpacking trip in the high country of Colorado. This was truly an inspirational mental rejuvenation. Jeff and I pitched our pup tent near a big snow bank several of the nights, ate delicious cut-throat trout, and had many days of leisure to just soak up the beauties of spruce and fir trees and wildlife.

When it was later announced that Helen and I would get married I had the vague hope, aside from the possible rejuvenation of my own life, that the marriage would possibly bridge the gap in my boys' lives. Helen was the same age as Ruth and had a son near my own sons' ages, whom they knew. Whatever the ultimate result may have been, the simultaneous disintegration of my family, as they sought their own destinies, was like a cosmic explosion. They went away, both near and far: Alan to Columbia, S.C., then Eugene, Oregon, and finally to the South Pacific to become an archaeologist; Steve to Swannanoa, N.C. for college; David to Washington, D.C. for work in government; Mike to Penn State for graduate study; and Jeff to Atlanta, Georgia, then to Eugene, Oregon for more college. Helen's son, Tim Sisk, also went away to college in Columbia, S.C. They all have had exceptionally successful careers, and the joy of seeing their lives unfold exceeds by far any others of my life.

Among various trips I was making in connection with research and professional meetings, Helen and I were fortunate to be able to travel to Europe in exchange for promoting a travel agency among friends and acquaintances, and several times we traveled in a program initiated by *Southern Living* magazine sponsoring trips to visit noted gardens. One of their sales attractions was to invite professors from southern universities, with their wives, to accompany groups and provide answers to horticultural questions during the tours.

The first trip, over two thousand miles, was from Amsterdam to Rome and return by a different route. A notable feature was a visit to Holland's decennial International Horticultural Exhibition, a breathtaking ten-acre exhibit located both indoors and out. Another memorable feature of this area at Aalsmeer, visited on another trip, was the world's largest flower auction: thirty-eight acres under one roof with five auction rings going simultaneously. The upside-down Dutch auction system begins with a high value and drops until the unit is sold; it is designed to ensure that all the perishable flowers are sold each day, with many going by air to the United States.

A European contrast with our cities was noted by many of our travelers in the many public-street flower markets. My own observation from the visits we made, and a source of constant inspiration to me, is that there are great gardens and landscapes, at modest and stately homes as well as castles, all over Europe. The beauties of flowers and nature in general are themes that can constitute a significant place in anyone's understanding the philosophy of Naturalism.

A reflection from all of these trips is that this art form must have originated, at least in the last few centuries and in its Western form, primarily in England and then spread to other European countries. The various gardens in England we visited (Kew, Castle Howard, Stourhead, Blenheim Palace, Hidcote, Bodmin, Shipley, Chatsworth, and others) are only a small fraction of the total. But we should not be so smug as to feel that great gardens could have originated only in the English mind. In Germany the island of Minau was originated by Swedish efforts. In Spain we visited the Alhambra and saw what incredible imagination the Moors had in bringing water by aqueduct from many miles away to sustain beautiful flowers and create pools and the sound of water falling in their gardens.

Coincidentally, our trip to Spain, as well as many others to Europe, broadened my knowledge as well as my philosophical outlook on history, as our guides often were college graduates majoring in the subject. For the two-week period of our trip, the guides described each place in the context of the entire history of the country. One little tidbit was "discovering" that the importance of the year 1492 in our American childhood school experience—Columbus's landing in America—was minor for our hosts. For the Spanish, 1492 mattered because it was on this date the Moors were finally run out of their country. In the fascinating city of Toledo it was sad to realize that three great religions had flourished and existed in harmony for generations—until 1492, the beginning of the infamous Inquisition, which exiled or killed many great intellectual figures of the time. To me the irony illuminated the crisis caused by the collision of faith with reason.

Several trips to Italy, Greece, and Switzerland clarified our comprehension of many realities in the advances of Western cultures. To actually stand on historical sites, go into great cathedrals, mosques, and synagogues, to see the ruins of the Parthenon, the Roman Coliseum, and various monuments to Reformation "heroes"—Luther, Calvin, Zwingli, Knox, and others—gave dimension to understanding that words fail to supply. Many times I have said (or quoted someone), "a picture is worth a thousand words, and a visit is worth a thousand pictures." I hope I live long enough to see some of the other four continents!

Behind the Iron Curtain

Of all my trips to professional meetings in Europe there was one with unusual excitement, as I was able to have Michael join me afterward for a ski trip to Austria. In 1983 I received an invitation to present a paper on my plant-environment research at a Symposium on Biophysics of Plant Systems in East Germany. In those days travel "behind the Iron Curtain" was permitted, but it was thought of as something less than comfortable given all the political tension between countries. The scheduled site of this meeting—the castle of Reinhardsbrunn near Gotha, Thuringia—could be reached by train from Frankfurt, where I arrived by plane during an unusually chilly March. On this cloudy day the train ride was rather grim and cheerless, particularly at the border-crossing stop. Military persons with long black coats came through checking tickets and credentials and trying to identify everyone. They took my passport and left for what seemed an interminable time. I was concerned that the long pause would jeopardize my connections with two other little local trains that ran only on a daily basis. Finally they came back, grudgingly returned the passport, and we set forth.

Since I was traveling alone, and was, in fact, the only symposium participant from the U.S., I brought detailed maps to make sure I could recognize all the towns where train changes should be made. I managed to make all my connections, though the rides were dismal and the cars dirty and somewhat crowded with obviously poor, shabbily dressed people. It was getting late in the day and I peered anxiously through the window to read all the signs (in German, of which I am supposed to have reading knowledge), so I was never quite sure of where we were. Eventually, a conductor came into my car and pronounced "Reinhardsbrunn." Struggling with two sizable suitcases, I climbed down and went into the small, forlorn, empty wooden depot with hardly a soul in sight, not even a counter with agent. On through the building I proceeded to the street side and found no one, no taxi, bus, or, as I hoped, someone from the symposium there to meet participants. There were no buildings or houses nearby, and the gravel road definitely identified Reinhardsbrunn as a rural location. I went back inside, looking for some poster or bulletin-board instructions. I even went back out the track-side door and actually found a little hand-written (cursive) note, obviously important; though much of the German was beyond my understanding, I still could recognize "symposium."

Returning to the street side I discovered a man coming past the station and ran to him to ask directions. He tried desperately but could not understand me. Then I went back and brought the hand-written note to him. He brightened up and, with many hand gestures, pointed up the road and (I think) explained it was only a little way and could be reached on foot. I thanked him profusely, we parted and I contemplated—what to do?

As it was late in the afternoon, the sky cloudy and beginning to get dark, and no phone booth or transportation in sight, I—what else—picked up my two heavy bags and trudged up the road into the woods, hoping to find the way. After perhaps a hundred yards, around a slight bend in the road, I saw a gap on one side of the road with a path into the woods. On a tree was a small notepaper with a simple hand-drawn arrow on it. Briefly I was quite relieved—this *had* to be the way. With new vigor I struck off down the path. At first this was fine, but after another hundred and fifty yards, winded, breaking into a sweat, the sky almost dark, I realized it was beginning to snow. I was in the middle of the forest with absolutely nothing in sight; I sat down on my bags to rest and consider what to do.

My silent conversation—"How in hell did I get in this situation?"—led to contemplation of my fate—"Will they find me frozen in the forest?" And I thought, "USC fans will really get a laugh at the headline, 'Clemson Professor Lost....'"

Gritting my teeth, I stood up and resolved to keep going. Suddenly through the trees ahead the silhouette of a building came into faint view, with a pointed tower-like structure on the roofline. Quickly I got out the program outline they had mailed and compared the roofline with the half-tone cover drawing. This is it!!!

With renewed vigor I plunged ahead, only to realize there was not a light or sound coming from the huge structure. Meanwhile, snowflakes were now very large and the ground almost white. Approaching in the dim light I could see a great oaken door with heavy iron hinges. I thought, "What am I supposed to do? Knock?" Not being able to bring myself to this humility, I picked up the bags and decided to at least circle the castle for further ideas. On the other side I saw two moving figures in the distance. Cautiously I approached and explained my problem. Luckily they could understand me and, in fact, were also attending the symposium (down the road in a hotel another half-mile farther) and had gone for a walk after dinner. It turned out that the castle administrators from the park service had been bogged in red tape and failed to send a timely notice of its closing for urgently needed renovations. So I plodded on to the hotel, found my good friend Arne, from Norway, with whom I had agreed to share a room, enjoyed a few beers, and laughed over the adventure.

The tower at Schloss Reinhardsbrunn

The three-day meeting, attended by more than one hundred research scientists (one or two from each European country and the rest from Russian universities and institutes) was very interesting. They gave my paper a very good reception and indicated intense interest in my methodology for quantifying daily growth of cereals, principally wheat, using the Haun scale, as it came to be named later. This recognition was in sharp contrast to the rather indifferent reception my work had received in fifteen previous years throughout the U.S.

One of the values of scientific endeavor is that researchers can share information without regard to other considerations, such as politics. But during the Cold War scientists and other personnel from behind the Iron Curtain were encouraged to gather as much information as possible from their Western counterparts—not just about our research but about life in the West. I was perhaps naïve about such practices, though the topic arose in a joking manner during this particular symposium.

Though I didn't know it at the time, the German organizer of the conference had safeguarded against repercussions for holding such an international symposium by ensuring that his co-sponsor was a member of the Communist party—a professor at Alexander von Humbolt University in Berlin and thus beyond criticism, if not suspicion. Ironically, almost thirty years later, at Christmas of 2010, I received a letter from my Norwegian friend that demonstrated that the concern about Stasi spying was no joke. (Stasi was the common short name for "Staatssicherheit," or State Security, the East German secret police.) He wrote:

> Dear Joe,
>
> Your enclosure to the Christmas greeting one year ago reminded me about a story from our visit in former GDR that I should have told you a long time ago. You probably remember K. U., ... the organiser of the symposium [who] had invited me in 1983....
>
> The reason for no [German-Norwegian] visits in the 1970s was simply that contact to the West was not allowed by the head of the [East German] institution. A couple of years after his retirement he was allowed a visa, and in 1987 he came to Norway for a couple of weeks....
>
> I do not know whether you remember the incident at the dinner table the evening when we just had arrived to the hotel where we lived. One of the servants informed us that only four persons were allowed to sit at the same table at the same time, but K. U. got quite upset and neglected the "order." Furthermore, we joked about who might be the Stasi agent at the arrangement.
>
> In the middle of the symposium week we had a social evening with a banquet, [after which] the institute's two secretaries came to us and invited us for a bottle of wine, which we consumed at their hotel room. I remember my busy time as interpreter from German to English and the other way, and I remember that the two ladies were most interested in hearing about America and life over there. However, we also heard a little about Germany, especially what took place in Berlin in 1945 when the Soviet troops arrived there. Daily life in GDR was not a topic.
>
> K. U. ...[told me that] after the symposium he had been ordered to go to Berlin and respond to the report from the Stasi agent at the symposium. The report had

accused him of using too much time on contact with participants from the western countries and too little on fellows from the socialistic countries....

The agent (reporter) was the younger of the two ladies who invited us to share a bottle of wine with them... She had been divorced some years earlier, and her daughter had fled from GDR to West Germany. In this situation, K. U. said, Stasi very easily could coerce her to be a reporter.... I have heard more dramatic stories about Stasi [using] people in a more or less difficult situation to make them reporters to the secret police.

Arne also notes that for several years after the symposium he received postcards from the same young lady, always from places in the Soviet Union where she had been on vacation. He wondered if she felt safe sending a card from a foreign country, but not from her own. He also informed me that our symposium host, K. U., had told him in Norway, "This bottle she has not paid by herself." Both Arne and I still relish the thought that the East German Secret Service spent money on a very expensive bottle of wine for us—one that their agent certainly could not afford—but still failed to entice a new agent on the western side of the Iron Curtain!

On one day of the symposium I joined an excursion for a few participants to visit Eisenach a few miles away. The main attraction is the massive, historic Wartburg Castle, located on a high hill with its walls set atop large cliffs; it is where Martin Luther hid in 1521 after his excommunication, and where he translated the Bible into German. We were able to visit the little room where he worked. His motivation, we were told, was a desire to have something common people could understand, in contrast to the obligatory Latin in use almost everywhere. Many years ago I had asked my father why Catholic services were always in Latin, and he answered it was "probably so most of

The wing of the Wartburg Castle where Luther translated the Bible

the parishioners could *not* understand and simply be enchanted and led by the mystical pontifical sounds." Though not presently much in sympathy with the theology of later Protestant ideologies proliferating around the world, I do think Luther made a bold and courageous act, and I was pleased to stand on the very spot where it happened.

The return train trip to Munich, on a sunny day, was not so grim as my arrival. It is probably fortunate that the trip was not made a few years later, just prior to the fall of the Berlin Wall. My travel would have been not far from Leipzig, where thousands were arrested while staging protests against the late, but not lamented, German Democratic Republic.

I met Mike at the Munich airport, and we rented a car and drove through Innsbruck, south over the 630-foot high Europa Bridge, to the little ski resort town of Neustift high in the Austrian Alps. There we had an elegant room for five days, thanks to one of the agents responsible for our many European garden tours. Each day we would drive up, park, and ride the huge lift fifteen hundred feet up to the foot of the Stubai glacier; from there other lifts radiated in several directions up to the crest of the mountain and the Italian border. There were no trees in sight, just a breathtaking expanse of snow for miles. Crevasses were well marked with flags where you dare not go.

I stuck to beginner and intermediate runs, while Mike was much more daring on the expert ones. We had great fun until the last day: on the very last run down a rather gentle slope to the top of the big lift, someone speeding out of control suddenly crashed into me from behind and knocked me completely out of my skis. As I slowly regained my senses I realized my left arm was numb and felt burned as if in scalding water, and I could not move my fingers. Though it seemed my arm was probably broken, the feeling gradually came back. Mike helped me to my skis and we made it back to the hotel. Medical examinations later indicated a nerve in my upper spine had been severely damaged; happily I recovered in several months.

In connection with one of my research projects financed by grant funds, I applied for a six-month sabbatical to make plant-growth observations in England, Norway, and Germany. The respective research institutions at Long Ashton, Ås, and Munich planted plots in advance of my arrival, found housing for Helen and me, and provided an assistant to train for making observations when I could not be present. At each location the professional associates were extremely cordial, and we visited many beautiful and historic places near each research center.

The time factor was helpful by enhancing the many glimpses of brief past visits and literary references that had touched our fancies in the past: in Bristol, near where we lived, the well-preserved Llandoger Trow pub where Robert Louis Stevenson wrote *Treasure Island*; across the Severn in Wales, Tintern Abbey—with no roof, thanks to Henry VIII. We occasionally attended sermons or performances in beautiful cathedrals: a black visiting minister in Westminster; the London Symphony in Wells (the acoustics are amazing in these huge masonry structures); and on a recurring basis the organ and choir music and sermons in Bristol Cathedral, nostalgic witness to dying embers of Christian crusading zealotry.

In Norway, we enjoyed our quaint cottage high on a hill above the Oslo fjord with a view of great ocean cruise ships, hearing engines throb day and night. We also visited the resistance museum depicting heroic acts of countless brave people during German occupation, the sod-roofed cabin where Ibsen wrote some of his plays, and the research plots of my close friend and associate, high above the timberline for the improvement of cattle pasture. In both Norway and England the enjoyable native foods and congenial associations with new friends greatly enriched our visits.

The "Leisure" of Retirement

My retirement from Clemson soon involved a change of scenery and joint efforts with Steve to build our homes in North Carolina. After his graduation from Warren Wilson College, Steve decided to stay around Asheville and develop a landscaping business. He soon discovered some beautiful forest land for sale on the mountainside with a grand view of the Swannanoa River valley and mountains in the distance. I helped financially, and subsequently we divided the twenty-five-acre plot so that two houses could be built. Along with our new neighbors we arranged a very desirable set of residential restrictions for preservation of natural features and future protection from undesirable development.

Having enjoyed successfully building two houses already, I now found, in the freedom of retirement, that helping Steve and Anne build their house, and another for us, was a delightful prospect. We began with his house, but since he was occupied with his landscape business and could work only on evenings and weekends, I commuted from Clemson for a period of months to work on the site, make arrangements for subcontractors, order materials, and supervise whatever operations Steve did not have time for.

After we had his house framed and roofed, a grand and momentous interlude took place! Steve and Anne (Squires) were married; the ceremony took place by a pool in the woods nearby, and the reception in the unfinished living room. A few months later, after final inspections, they happily moved in. In the last phases of their construction I arranged for advance roadway and site grading for our house so that construction could begin as soon as possible.

Stone Work

On Steve and Anne's house I was able to fulfill a long-anticipated desire to do stone masonry. Enlarging on what were probably hereditary (or poverty-induced) factors that stimulated or demanded do-it-yourself work, I did everything from surveying, hand digging, carpentry, plumbing, painting, and, at last, block- and stonemasonry. As a teenager at the Homesteads I remember being entranced by the stonemasons and experimenting with piling stones for dry-stack stone terraces at our place. On the rocky mountainside where we were building, we optimistically visualized early on, since stones for building were everywhere in our woods, that all we had to do was "pick 'em up." This worked fine for a lot of terrace retaining walls, but sadly it turned to a misguided assumption later, as we realized the stones could not be stacked vertically without huge ugly mortar joints between them.

My interest in stonework had been whetted a few years earlier (while we were still living at Clemson) by an experience during one of my consulting trips to England. I managed to spend a few days down in the Cotswold Hills of Gloucestershire with Ruth's cousin, a retired attorney, and his wife, who lived in a historic antique—an approximately hundred-fifty-year-old stone house called Draycot. The back yard was surrounded by a massive four-foot stone fence, and I noticed an irregular opening at one place where it had been pulled down, apparently many years before, leaving stones strewn about. Perhaps a hunter had been looking for a rabbit hiding in the many cozy spaces under the wall. Wanting to do something around the house to repay my hosts for all their kindness, I asked if they planned to restore the fence to its original state.

"Well yes," he said, "but I haven't found a restoration mason just yet."

Guessing I could do the job in a few hours, I asked if they would mind if I tried. "Oh no, we would not think of letting you do that sweaty job." Knowing they were very particular about all the priceless antiques in their house, I guessed that they were being very cautious of my work. But after much discussion of how stones had to be positioned very carefully, with weathered sides on the surface and the varying sizes placed in appropriate harmony with the existing parts, they agreed that I could go ahead. The final result was successful beyond my expectations: you could not tell where the replaced section was located.

From then on I had complete confidence in my stonework. However, as my knowledge of professional masonry (with mortar) was limited, we thought immediately of Helen's brother, an expert semi-retired brick- and block-mason who, we realized, could do some of our work while training me as well. Thomas had a jovial, fun-loving spirit and was a constant psychological lift to the otherwise heavy demanding work. He accomplished the required "plumbness," spacing, and mortar qualities required by building codes, all of which I dutifully learned at his elbow. Then came the stonework itself, about which he was also quite knowledgeable, from seeing and helping close relatives who were masons. He had great admiration for the work and knew the methods, but he didn't relish doing it as I did. Still, he helped me get started.

Quality stonemasonry requires considerable imagination in selecting shapes and positions of the stones to create a sense of randomness and avoid monotony. Also, the mortar is entirely different from brick and block mortar, with less plasticity but still flexible enough to conform to irregular stone surfaces without oozing out between courses, as in brick masonry. Every mason develops his own taste or judgment for the finished appearance. For most large commercial jobs, the mason even has to build a sample wall near the building site to demonstrate the effect proposed. Aside from the

Draycot before

obvious problem of needing sufficient imagination to select shapes that will fit each spot to produce a homogenous result as one builds upward—large and small intermingled—is the need to recess mortar between stones, using as little as possible to keep joints small and create an illusion of mortarless dry-wall construction.

My first efforts were on Steve's walls covering the foundation blocks. We plunged ahead, assuming the local stones we had collected would work, but quickly discovered, to my immense disappointment, they were entirely unsuitable. Most were too round or oval to fit in any sensible way. After much panic, my thoughts cycling back to the facings of walls I had considered attractive stone work, I realized you have to use stones with edges, that is, more square or rectangular. Next we looked up places in the area that supplied stone wholesale to builders, went to look, and discovered that types with color and shape we liked actually were shipped from close to where I had lived in Tennessee, and had been used on the house I had lived in at the Homesteads. Possibly just a coincidence of artistic good fortune or, more likely, an example of cultural evolution—selecting something subconsciously known from youth.

There were still decisions to make. The sandstone involved could be obtained as quarried and cut into symmetrically regular pieces, or we could get "field" or "woods" stones, still with perceptible edges, weathered and moss- or lichen-covered. We preferred the latter to produce a more rustic appearance. The price including delivery was reasonable, and we eventually ordered over a hundred tons.

When using most types of stone, it is necessary to break off parts with a stone hammer and chisel to fit them into the space of the veneer desired. The main characteristic of my work—to create a total overall rustic appearance—was to place each stone so that the weathered, non-broken surface was visible on the finished surface and any broken part hidden inside.

With the Tennessee field sandstone the work went much better with the results we desired. In addition to the foundation wall, I built the fireplace, with Thomas helping me follow the engineering

Draycot after

plans very carefully, using correct fire-brick liners, heat-resistant mortar, damper, flue liners, and above all, tight glass doors to close at night, preventing heat loss up the chimney from the living space. The fireplace satisfied our lifelong appreciation for this constant winter cheer—and brought considerable savings in heating costs, with a limitless store of wood from our forest.

We designed and positioned the houses to incorporate many other aspects of energy conservation: orienting them with the large areas of thermo-pane windows facing south; six-inch wall studs, instead of the usual four-inch, thus providing one-third more space for insulation; twice the usual attic insulation; a deep roof overhang to reduce the amount of sunlight hitting floors during summer, but allowing maximum contact during winter; Styrofoam thermal barriers under cement tile floor slabs; heat-pump cooling/heating systems. All these features resulted in considerable energy savings as compared to average consumption of equal-sized houses.

Building from the ground up

Having built Steve's foundation walls and fireplace, I was ready to attack my place. A bit more aspiring, though not willing to do the entire exterior in stone, I decided to have large spaces twenty feet high and twelve feet horizontally around each corner of the house, each requiring about fifteen tons of masonry.

After building my chimney and fireplace, the last phase of my masonry life came with the installation of floor tile. Steve had opted for a professional masonry instructor, a personal friend, to do his floor with conventional commercial tile. Wanting to economize even further, I negotiated with Steve's mason to come and teach me how to do it. Further, we had found that Mexican tile, with a desirable rustic appearance we liked, was much more expensive due to its time-consuming installation cost. It was clear that because the tile itself was quite affordable, if I could install it myself, it would be

The fireplace

feasible. The process comprised many stages and took many weeks, and not only was it interesting to learn, but it produced a very desirable result.

For twenty years our life in this house was a constant joy—great mountain views, quiet solitude, flowers and gardens, birds, wildflowers, hiking, and cutting firewood from fallen trees in our own forest, interspersed with travel and various social and civic activities. We also had much time for reading, studying, enriching our lives through learning and recapturing many things that should have been stowed away in college.

The stone corners of the author's house near Swannanoa, North Carolina

After a few years in the house we came to the realization it might be nice to adopt or somehow acquire some other creature to share our space. We had not had pets since the Clemson years so the next thought—"Why not get a dog?"—led us to fence part of the yard, cut a dog-door into the garage, put a cozy bunk-bed under the work bench…and then set forth to find one. At first our interest centered on purebred Labrador pups; then, coming to more rational thoughts, we realized many desperate friendless dogs in rescue shelters needed homes. After considerable search we came to a pen with several wildly barking dogs of various breeds. One stood slightly back, not barking but looking up with that friendliness characteristic of a Lab. He sent pleading looks toward us, and we both wanted him immediately. We took him out for a walk and realized he was the answer to our dream.

We took his name from a cruise trip to Baja California, Mexico, where we had visited "Cabo San Lucas"; Helen had said that last word would be a good name for a pet. For the next eight years Lucas was our ever-loving companion. So many things were imprinted in our lives, never to be forgotten. After only three days we had to leave him, for just a few hours, in his "secure" back yard; when we came back he had dug out under one of the gates, torn down two of our screen doors to the house (obviously trying to get *in* rather than run away), and was wildly overjoyed to see us return. Subsequently, as my shadow, he would not sleep in his bunk, nor would a comfortable pad by the fireplace suffice. For a night or two I tried having him sleep on my bed. Sadly this did not work as he chose the middle of the bed, softly growling when I tried to nudge him over. From then on he reconciled himself to a nice pad next to my bed, and for years he went eagerly with me on hour-long daily walks up on the mountain ridge above our house.

Another early incident was a trip to the kennel to which he reluctantly agreed. After this ten-day imprisonment, the kennel owners reported, "He had a very unsettled, barking stay." When I got him into the car he sat very close and furiously licked my ear while I drove home. After several more kennel visits he became adjusted to them—possibly he enjoyed visits with other dogs—well enough that he would leave my ear alone on the return trips.

Though I had had many pet dogs all through my life, enjoying them greatly, I had never gotten to a real appreciation of their sense of possible understanding of other creatures, particularly humans, or, above all, their potential concern for others. Lucas's behavior, companionship, and intensely enjoyable personality led me to quite a bit of biological *cum* philosophical questioning. I thought back to graduate school and the studies Konrad Lorenz had made on animal and human behavior. From the countless examples of animals' seemingly human perceptions and responses among widely differing species, I found it quite logical to assume dogs have the same essence, or "soul," as humans. For that matter, all animals *could* have that quality.

"Soul" Work

Most animals, unlike plants and inanimate objects, rely on control centers that regulate behaviors for survival, pleasure, creativity, and many other physical and mental activities that enrich their existence. The brain has the capacity for *memory*, the storage of information, both perceived and imaginary, which can vary widely in its accuracy or reality. Also, it has the profound ability, through *imagination*, to assimilate this information into ideas, inventions, and other creative behaviors. The mind also relies on, and has to deal with, *instincts*, the familiar baggage of evolution that can be essential to survival ("flight" from danger) or very destructive ("fight" a perceived foe) if not understood and managed in a "civilized" way.

Overshadowing all this basic biology is the reality of cultural evolution, i.e., the way groups or societies can influence the actions and behavior of their members. For example, a basic feature of most religions is the effort to explain the great unanswered question of what happens to us after we die. Our "Judeo-Christian" culture has copiously rendered good and bad visions of the afterlife: images of "Heaven" and "Hell," to which we are exposed frequently from early childhood on, remain in the memory for the rest of one's life. Whether or not one believes in such an afterlife, whether one lives by faith that heaven and hell exist or by the knowledge that there is not one shred of scientific evidence for such places, the images remain.

A culture's historical experiences, its explanations for phenomena not understood, the typical search for a scapegoat when things go wrong—that is, its memories and imagination and instincts—often combine into a worldview that places a "spiritual" reality outside the realm of the real or physical world. That realm is impossible to prove or disprove, leaving it purely a matter of faith, which can be easily inculcated from generation to generation. This phenomenon—any culture's worldview of an imaginary, or "spiritual" realm—generally goes by the term "religion."

Some of the world's dominant religions are in well-earned disrepute for condoning violence, war, and many other forms of inhumane behavior. An example of this is the experience of Jill Carroll, a journalist captured and later released in war-torn Iraq in 2006, who witnessed the indoctrination of a small child being told of the great joy and salvation resulting from killing a Jew and/or an American. Such ideas can exist, and persist, only through that combination of memory (of some "other") and imagination into a collective "spirituality." The Nazi zeitgeist of racial purification reflected—and Auschwitz embodied—one culture's "spiritual" convictions, just as most, if not all, of Islamic terrorists' actions in the 1990s and 2000s have been motivated by the "spiritual" convictions of another culture.

As a result of such behaviors, terms such as "spirituality," when used to connote religiosity, can become pejorative simply by association. But I do not wish to imply that the *concept* of "spirituality" is bad. My own understanding of spirituality, though I lack a ready substitute for the word "religion," leads me to prefer "creative imagination." Here are a few dictionary definitions to consider in thinking about the words and the concepts:

> Imagination *n.* 1. the faculty or action of forming new ideas, or images or concepts of external objects not present in the senses;

2. the ability of the mind to be creative or resourceful; 3. the part of the mind that imagines things

Soul *n.* 1. the spiritual or immaterial part of a human being or animal, regarded as immortal; 2. identity or essence of something: "integrity is the soul of intellectual life" (*see p. xii for a more thorough definition*)

Spirit *n.* 1. the nonphysical part of a person that is the seat of emotions and character; 2. the part of a person that is capable of surviving death; 3. courage, energy, determination; 4. supernatural being and/or impressions of real people and animals

Spiritual *adj.* 1. of, relating to, or affecting the human spirit or soul as opposed to material or physical things; 2. of, or relating to, religious belief: "Iran's spiritual leader"

Spiritualism *n.* 1. a system of belief or religious practice based on supposed communication with the spirits of the dead; a philosophical doctrine that the spirit exists as distinct from matter, or that the spirit is the only reality

With a different approach, Gary Kowalski, in his book *The Souls of Animals*, describes animal attributes and behaviors, as well as his interpretation of them:

> ...animals share many human characteristics. They have emotional lives, experience love and fear, and possess their own integrity, which suffers when not respected. They play and are curious about their world. They develop loyalties and display altruism. To me, animals have all the traits indicative of soul. For soul is not something we can see or measure. We can only observe its outward manifestations: in tears and laughter, in courage and heroism, in generosity and forgiveness.... Soul is the point at which our lives intersect the timeless, in our love of goodness, our zest for beauty, our passion for truth."

Kowalski captures my own belief. I, too, think of the soul as the place where knowledge mixes with evolutionary instincts to create a desirable existence starkly in contrast to the primitive "savage" state. Everyone, I believe, has an urge to develop his or her own concept of religion, usually individualized within, or derived from, an existing faith community. My own leans toward a deep appreciation of, almost awe regarding nature, the universe, the creative results of imagination such as art, music, invention, literature, discovery, and other achievements that enrich life and society.

Community Work—Ethics in Politics

During our years on the mountain we also undertook other community and civic interests. I had long avoided participation in political activity, which I corrected by becoming active in the Buncombe County Democratic Party, subsequently as chairman of the precinct for several years. Despite the conservative slant of many members, it was rewarding to get to know many fellow residents of the county and the city of Asheville, and to see a gradual increase in the percentage of people voting.

My political activities naturally led me to intensive interest and extensive efforts on the subject of campaign finance reform. And, as a longtime Unitarian and more recent member of the Ethical Society of Asheville (affiliated with the Ethical Culture Society), my understanding of appropriate behavior in public life was informed by my own "spiritual" leanings.

Most religious liberals (or, perhaps, liberal Protestants and Jews), in the United States, including of course Unitarian-Universalists, firmly believe in the separation of church and state. And I would propose that the vast majority of UUs and Ethical Culturalists are politically active. But it still surprises me how reluctant liberal faith institutions are to address political ethics. Mention of the word "politics" immediately seems to suggest combining church and state in a way that is inappropriate for a Sunday service.

Mohandas Gandhi—the "Mahatma," or "great soul," unquestionably a religious leader who changed the political history of his country—asserted, "I can say without the slightest hesitation and yet in all humility, that those who say that religion has nothing to do with politics do not know what religion means." Certainly Dr. Martin Luther King, Jr., who did the same for our own democratic nation, would agree.

After all, the behavior of our lawmakers should be ethical, and encouraging ethical behavior falls clearly within the spiritual domain of the church. Conservative congregations have not hesitated in recent decades to speak out, often stridently, to influence elected officials' behavior; why should liberal ones not do the same? In my view, the teaching and preaching of churches about what is *ethical* behavior in public life should be broadened to include economic issues (e.g., a graduated income tax and minimum wage), universal access to affordable health care and quality education, and a host of other problems. If positions on these issues echo the stance of a party or candidate, that does not mean that the church is acting in a partisan fashion—rather, that the party or candidate is reflecting the values of that church or congregation.

My interest in this subject began with my first course in history and intensified in the early 1970s when I joined Common Cause, a nonpartisan organization whose goal is to ensure open, honest, and accountable government at the federal, state, and local levels. Some of its earliest efforts were to end U.S. involvement in Vietnam, challenge secrecy in government, promote nuclear arms control, and advance civil liberties and equal rights. Most prominent though, in recent years, has been Common Cause's leadership in the efforts to curb the influence of money in politics. An honest observer must acknowledge that political ethics reflect, in inverse proportion, the amount of money in politics.

During my forty-five years as a Unitarian I have never seen an issue calling out more for social action than money's influence over our political system. It not only corrupts the basic principles of democracy, but it undermines legislators' ability to honestly address the needs of their constitutents—and fellow humans—as well as the myriad problems we face including poverty, hunger, and healthcare. If we do not change the system, we are headed for a state of plutocracy, in which we are governed by a few wealthy people and powerful corporations instead of the votes of the people.

Although most people, particularly younger ones, think of our country as being fairly old or mature, in fact, our modern "democracy" represents just five percent of recorded history: 235 out of more than 5,000 years of record-keeping. And ours has never been an ideal, or "perfected" democracy. Slavery and sexism were enshrined in the Constitution and lasted ninety more years. Originally, only white male property owners could vote. For a century after the Civil War and Reconstruction, poll taxes and literacy requirements prevented African Americans in many states from voting, and women—even "white women with property"—could not cast a ballot until 1920. Only the Civil Rights laws and determined efforts in the 1960s and 1970s guaranteed the universal franchise in many southern states.

So why is it that now, even with earlier barriers to voting removed, scarcely half of all eligible voters bother to vote? The simple answer is cynicism, based on experience. Voters are disillusioned by the thought that the huge contributions of corporations and special-interest groups will win, the knowledge that *whoever is elected will seek to please those who furnished the money instead of the majority of voters*. Thus, many people just stay away from the polls.

Let me acknowledge that there are many instances of unethical behavior by government officials that don't involve the corrupting factor of money (at least directly, although profit usually lurks in the background). But whatever the profit to the officeholder, while there are short-term benefits to a few, the greater good, even the country as a whole, suffers in the long run. Some examples include:

- Andrew Jackson sanctioned the killing of Native Americans and encouraged their expulsion to the west, in order to expropriate their land for the use of white settlers. A century and a half elapsed before Native Americans began to be recompensed for their losses, and even today many reservations are beset by poverty, alcoholism, and other social pathologies, and Native Americans are second-, third-, or fourth-class citizens.
- When Theodore Roosevelt wanted to build the Panama Canal, the isthmus was part of Colombia. But negotiations for a treaty with Colombia became stalled, so his administration fabricated the story that Panama wished to secede and sign the treaty with the U.S., contacted individuals who would participate in a junta, and arranged for American gunboats to stand by to ensure the success of the plan.

While we gained the canal, we lost Latin America. In 1912 an American minister at Bogotá, James Du Bois, wrote, "By refusing to allow Colombia to uphold her sovereign rights over a treaty she had held for eighty years, the friendship of nearly a century has disappeared; and the indignation of every Colombian, and millions of other Latin Americans has been aroused. The confidence and trust in the justice and fairness of the U.S. has completely vanished." The validity of this indictment was substantiated in 1921 when President Woodrow Wilson initiated payment to Colombia of an indemnity of $25 million for the loss of Panama. It was further proven in 1959 when Vice President Richard Nixon's motorcade was stoned; and when United Fruit was nationalized in various countries (1945-54; 1974-76); and, most recently, when Venezuela underwent an anti-imperialist—read anti-American—revolution in 1998.

Jackson's and Roosevelt's unethical behavior did not reward them with money, but with power and influence. In the early days of our country the influence of money in politics was relatively unimportant because the population was small and only a fraction of the populace was permitted to vote. It was only toward the end of the 19th century, when large corporations, or "trusts," were first sanctioned by the courts, that the corrupting influence of money began to be felt (and, ironically, Teddy Roosevelt made his reputation as the "trustbuster").

In some eras since then, reforms have been put in place to curb the influence of money, and in others its power has been allowed or encouraged to flourish. One thinks of the Gilded Age (1875-1905), the "Roaring '20s," and the "Greed is Good" decades since 1980; and, conversely, Theodore Roosevelt's trust-busting (1901-1908), the banking reforms of Franklin Roosevelt's New Deal (1933-1940), and the attempts at reform of Lyndon Johnson's Great Society (1965-1968). Sadly, whenever reforms are established, whatever form they take, new ways are found to circumvent them. A few recent examples of successful, corporate-financed influence:

- Wine sales—A wine company provided $5.1 million for the USDA to promote exports of its products.
- Mountaintop removal—Coal companies override EPA rulings to dump Appalachian mountaintop debris into rivers and streams, by buying the support of governors, congressmen, senators, and judges. Profits go out of state while poverty and coal- and pollution-induced illnesses impact local residents.
- Ethanol—Despite Treasury Department estimates that tax

credits for the ethanol industry have cost taxpayers $5.9 billion in lost revenues, credits and direct subsidies support corporate investments in ethanol production. The desire for "cleaner-burning ethanol fuels" is undercut by the fact that ethanol is an energy-negative process, i.e. its production takes more energy (from coal, gas, or oil with attendant air pollution) than it will produce when burned. Furthermore, the increased levels of fertilizer used in growing corn for ethanol flow through the entire Mississippi River basin to create a vast dead zone in the Gulf of Mexico, destroying the Gulf's fishing industry, which, confined to three or four relatively poor states, has far less political influence than the hugely profitable agribusiness industry spanning the Midwest. By 2011, the use of corn for ethanol production so diminished the amount available for food or animal feed that worldwide price increases were seen in everything from breakfast cereal to pork chops.

- S & L bailout—One of the worst financial disasters (before Enron) of the country was closely linked to campaign contributions that caused legislators to ignore early warning signs. It eventually cost the taxpayers $1.4 trillion dollars.
- Pharmaceutical drug prices—Senators and representatives take large contributions from companies that get extensions on their drug patents, thus keeping off the market generic drugs—the less expensive equivalents preferred by millions of people—and increasing profits by hundreds of billions of dollars. In legislation establishing the Medicare prescription law of 2003, the pharmaceutical lobby, PharMa, inserted prohibitions against the government negotiating for lower prices or re-importing drugs from Canada.
- The Military-Industrial complex—Since the end of World War II this nexus of the Defense Department and American corporations has operated beyond the control of, and without any meaningful oversight by, any civilian authority. The

military services make sure to spread weapons programs across hundreds of congressional districts and to farm out cost-plus contracts to thousands of influential businesses, ensuring political support—and limitless financing for political supporters—for whatver they want. Military and corporate largesse also flows to think tanks and universities to ensure intellectual and academic cover for the weapons systems and other projects the services and corporations wish to undertake.

It takes a great amount of money to run for office, and usually the candidate with deeper pockets wins. More than three billion dollars were spent in the election cycle of 2008; the average Senate candidate spent nearly $4 million. Unfortunately, small contributors are discouraged from giving when they realize what vast amounts are coming from corporations and special interest groups. It has been reported that 90 percent of the money comes from less than one percent of the population. Obviously the big contributors expect something for their contributions. I will cite a few examples from Martin Schram's book, *Speaking Freely*, in which former members of Congress tell of their experiences and feelings:

- When Senator Wyche Fowler (Georgia) sat on the Ways and Means Committee for six years, many special interest groups sought to be subsidized by changes in the tax code. "I am sure that on many occasions—I'm not proud of it—I made the choice that I needed the big corporate client and therefore I voted for, or sponsored a provision, even though I did not think that it was in the best interests of the country or the economy."
- Senator Pete Kostmayer (Pennsylvania): "It's (often) not what you do, but what you don't do (that is wrong). In something like NAFTA, if you're a Democrat and you've gotten support from labor but you don't like labor's position on it (but think it is going to pass anyway), you just keep quiet about it."
- Rep. Tim Penny (Minnesota): "Sometimes there are high-priority items of special interest groups who gave you money. You disagree with these items on principle. But since there

is no chance that they are going to pass you vote for them anyway. Those are the votes to this day that I wish I had not cast. Thankfully, the bills never went anywhere. They died in the Senate."

Lawmakers also consider the time required for raising money a huge problem in financing elections:
- Sen. George Mitchell (Maine): "Almost every day in the six years I was Majority Leader, one or more senators called and asked me not to have a vote at a certain time because they were either holding or attending a fund-raising event."
- Rep. Thomas Downey (N.Y.): "How is the process compromised by money? Well, because a good portion of your time is spent raising it as opposed to doing the things you were elected to do."

As soon as lawmakers arrive in Washington they usually seek assignments to the committees of their choice, called "cash cows." These assignments virtually guarantee that members will have no difficulty raising money, because it will come from the special interests whose fates are decided by the committees. Many lawmakers actively solicit contributions from groups whose special interests are regulated by their committee. They think nothing of it—but the public, *with an innate sense of ethics*, views this common practice as little more than legal solicitation of bribes. Lawmakers defend the practice by claiming that "money doesn't buy votes," only access. And access is probably the most direct route to receiving favorable action. One congressman described it this way: "You receive far more requests for appointments than you can handle...so you may ask a staff assistant to see someone. Then the assistant says, 'Well he did give $10,000 to your campaign.' And the congressman then says, 'Oh, well, I better see him then.'"

How similar that is to a story a Catholic friend told me! A lady had visited her priest to tell him how sad she was that her dog had died, and that she was so attached to the pet that she would like the priest to say mass for its funeral. The priest said he was very sorry but he usually did not say mass for animals. As she turned away, the lady said, "I was thinking of giving $1,000 in the pet's name to the church." To which the priest responded, "Oh, that's different. I didn't realize he was Catholic."

In 2002 we took heart from the enactment of the McCain-Feingold bill, which attempted to ban "soft money"—the massive amounts of unregulated contributions flowing into political parties from corporations, labor unions, and wealthy individuals. Before the ink was dry on the new law, plots were underway to set up front groups to serve as conduits for soft money. And now the Federal Election Commission has voted *to allow them to do it*—as long as the front groups were created before the law took effect. In numerous lawsuits in the years following its passage, the Supreme Court upheld almost every restriction of McCain-Feingold. But in January 2010, in *Citizens United*, the Supreme Court—reconstituted with extremely partisan Republicans by the Bush administration—gutted the restrictions, overturned a century of precedent, and proclaimed that corporations (and unions, though their resources are one-hundredth of corporate money) can give unlimited amounts to candidates.

There is a way around the political games, stalling, and loopholes standing in the way of real reform. It is called "Clean Money" and it is very simple. Candidates who agree to forgo private contributions and accept spending limits get public funds for their campaigns. It is already working in Maine, Vermont, Arizona, and Massachusetts, and seventeen other states are considering similar approaches. Under this system, a candidate must collect a small contribution and signature from a minimum number, or fixed proportion, of voters to obtain public funding. This will permit qualified persons to run for office without having to have great wealth. And when they are elected, they will not be beholden to the moneyed interests but instead can do the things for which they were elected, rather than having to raise more money to become reelected.

Another desirable step would be to provide free television time for legitimate candidates and prohibit paid campaign commercials. For decades Britain has banned paid political ads in national elections, requiring the BBC and its commercial rivals to make free time available to candidates. The airwaves are publicly owned, and cable-casting is regulated by franchise agreements with local governments; there is no reason that private companies profiting from the public communication channels should not be required to give back in the form of free airtime.

For decades in North Carolina, elected judges solicited campaign contributions from trial lawyers who appear before them. When a lawyer acting on behalf of large corporate interests argues a case of little or marginal interest to the general public (and, perhaps, of questionable connection to existing statutes or constitutional precedent), and the presenting lawyer has contributed $15,000 to the campaign of the judge hearing the case, how objective can that judge be? To address this type of conflict, the state legislature passed laws providing public financing for candidates for Supreme Court and Appellate Court, state Auditor, Insurance Commissioner, and Superintendent of Education; in future years public financing is expected to cover all judicial offices. This historic reform, acknowledged as the most sweeping campaign finance reform in the country, began to be copied in thirteen other states. In 2011, however, the state legislature, led by Republican majorities for the first time in in 140 years, passed legislation to remove all public financing from elections and return judicial races to a partisan basis; only a veto by the Democratic governor could preserve this important reform.

While no laws can guarantee the integrity of lawmakers, it is quite possible to eliminate the most profound cause and most direct source of unethical behavior among elected officials: the huge infusions of special-interest money into politicians' campaign coffers.

If public officials ever become determined to regain oversight and control over their own actions, they might someday reach for the magic wand, wave it, and discover that they indeed have the power to make special-interest money vanish from the political process. Legislators in Maine, Vermont, Massachusetts, Arizona, and in no small way in North Carolina, show that it is possible to eliminate, or at least minimize, the subversive influence of money on politics.

Why this long detour into politics and ethics, the nature of soul and spirit? My life had passed through a period of profound change with the loss of my first wife, the dispersal of my family, and my retirement from a long, satisfying career. In midlife I began to reconstruct myself, with a new marriage, relocation to Western North Carolina, and activities that, in retrospect, are all of a piece—hand-crafting homes for my son and me, learning new skills, and addressing questions that, in essence, are all one: What is this life all about?

IMAGINE

Imagine there's no heaven
It's easy if you try
No hell below us
Above us only sky
Imagine all the people
Living for today...

Imagine there's no countries
It isn't hard to do
Nothing to kill or die for
And no religion too
Imagine all the people
Living life in peace...

You may say I'm a dreamer
But I'm not the only one
I hope someday you'll join us
And the world will be as one

Imagine no possessions
I wonder if you can
No need for greed or hunger
A brotherhood of man
Imagine all the people
Sharing all the world...

You may say I'm a dreamer
But I'm not the only one
I hope someday you'll join us
And the world will live as one

John Lennon

The Search for Truth

While my search for truth has been a lifelong quest, it was the terrorist bombings of September 11, 2001 that forged my occasional musings and decades of wonderings into the single question, "Why?" Why do people behave as they do? What underlies not just our human impulses but our humanity per se? In this section I have sought to identify some central, fundamental truths that have helped me make sense of this phenomenon we so readily enjoy but so little apppreciate—a conscious, conscientious, introspective life.

CHAPTER 9

IMAGINATION

A few weeks after the 9/11 attacks I came to my senses and made the following statement (also expressed by many other writers): "This ought to be a wake-up call for everyone." In my science-trained mind (or perhaps in childish simplicity) I asked myself, "Why would several college-educated men who were, presumably, intellectually informed, intentionally take their own and thousands of other lives in such a fashion?" In other words, what could possibly motivate such action? The only rational answer I could find was—religion.

Subsequently, as I considered both the proximate and more abstract causes for that religious motivation (or fanaticism), I was forced to confront the most direct cause, in the Middle East: Israel's intransigence in continuing to settle "Arab" lands. So my immediate putative solution was (and after nine years still is) that the United States should withhold the vast subsidies it provides until Israel lives up to its signed and promised agreements to discontinue those settlements. Of course that has not happened; instead, the conflict has escalated, even intensified, by the unnecessary invasion of Iraq and further actions by Israel (more settlements in the West Bank, incursions into Gaza, etc.). And we still face fanatic would-be bombers and religion-driven mass murderers today.

As my thoughts progressed I was impelled to study philosophical "evolution" a bit to see if religion could really be such a simple (or complicated) culprit. Among the valuable sources I turned to for background knowledge were Will Durant's *The Story of Philosophy* and *The Truth About the Truth: De-confusing and Re-constructing the Postmodern World,* edited by Walter Truett Anderson. I also delved into a book by Theodosius Dobzhansky, a geneticist and evolutionist who immigrated to the United States in 1927 (when I was five years old) and taught at Caltech, Columbia, and Rockefeller Universities. His concept of the nature of religious thought, which he called "The Biology of Ultimate Concern," helped frame my own thinking.

First, a clarification about science and philosophy. Many people confuse the work of philosophers with that of scientists in search for the great truths of the universe. But in fact, scientists gather, study, and analyze data to build an understanding of how things work. They might or might not use that understanding to address larger issues or paint a more comprehensive picture of the world, but at its core their work focuses almost exclusively on the question of "how." And any explanation can be tested, over and over as new data comes to light, to see whether or not it still stands.

Philosophers address a different question: they try to understand *why* things work as they do. And, because there are no duplicable tests to prove or disprove an explanation as to why, there can be no end to the answers philosophers can come up with. Thus philosophers have been stumbling around for centuries to explain our world and our culture, reaching from Romanticism to Modernism, Existentialism, and finally to the absurd Postmodernism, which is the belief that Truth cannot be found. Postmodernism is the ultimate antithesis of the Enlightenment. The difference between the two can be expressed as follows: Enlightenment thinkers believed that we can eventually know everything, and radical postmodernists believe that we can know nothing.

In trying, myself, to understand how we came to this situation, I have come to realize that it is difficult for any rationalist to understand the more "advanced" philosophers, which is the reason I have gotten so much help from Durant's work.

To return to the scientific realm, where I might understand how our nature—our biology—might lead to such behavior: Dobzhansky's "ultimate concern" relates to all the attitudes or feelings normally associated with religion, i.e. beliefs in a god, or many gods, or other supernatural beings or forces as part of the "natural" world (however supernatural or unnatural they might be). His "ultimate concern" also tries to answer (though not using scientific method) questions of *how* our universe was created, and of *why* we and other creatures exist, and *why* we behave as we do. These are thus among the "ultimate" questions, as Paul Tillich earlier (1959) recognized in relating "ultimate concern" to the essence of religion.

Similarly, E. O. Wilson writes, "The predisposition to religious belief is the most complex and powerful force in the human mind and in all probability an ineradicable part of human nature…. Mankind has produced on the order of one hundred thousand religions." He observes that since the time of the Enlightenment, "Skeptics have continued to nourish the belief that science and learning will banish religion…." And yet, "The United States, technologically the most sophisticated nation in history, is also the second most religious—after India." It is obvious that human beings are still largely ruled by myth.

Myths

Myths are many things. They may be distortions of actual events, or fragments of dead religions, or the personification of philosophical or abstract ideas. The development of a myth is slow and unconscious and grows into acceptance as indisputable fact through scores of generations of telling and retelling.

Regardless of their origin, the myths of religious belief shape both modern and primitive peoples. They give shape and meaning to the

> It can also be helpful to approach philosophy with humor, as does Steven Katz in *How to Speak and Write Postmodern:*
>
> "The postmodern era has given us some really good ideas and some really bad writing. From Derrida on down to humble troopers in the trenches of academia, a style has come to prevail among postmodernists. It is one of endless complexification and obscurity. The general idea seems to be that the surest way to establish yourself as a profound thinker is to make it very difficult for anybody to understand what you are saying. This has the virtue, also, of protecting you against the possible discovery that you have nothing to say whatever."

randomness of life, often by offering "reward" and threatening "punishment" or enticing with the promise of good luck. As Wilson describes it, "Many primitive religions sought supernatural help for reward of long life, abundant land, and the avoidance of physical catastrophes and the defeat of enemies." Dobzhansky phrases it this way: "In every known human society people have arrived at some system of religious views concerning the meaning and the proper conduct of their lives. Religion enables human beings to make peace with themselves and with the formidable universe into which they are flung by some power greater than themselves."

But how can these myths have such power in a time when scientific knowledge explains the workings of the universe in a provable, testable way? Does it make sense, given our knowledge of reproduction, genetics, and fertility, that a woman might overcome "God's anger" and become pregnant—if she'll only crawl half a mile across the plaza to reach the Cathedral at Lourdes? Knowing how cyclonic systems function or how electricity is produced, how can modern man still imagine, in effect, Thor throwing thunderbolts and Aeolus blowing winds around the world?

As Wilson points out, "The enduring paradox of religion is that so much of its substance is demonstrably false, yet it remains the driving force in all societies. Human beings are absurdly easy to indoctrinate—they *seek* it." A close friend of mine characterizes our reliance on myth this way: "We so prefer to anthropomorphize the mystery of creation that we cook up beliefs in place of verified findings and plausible explanations of physical phenomena."

We are, as Ernest Becker describes us in *The Birth and Death of Meaning*, an "ego-controlled animal" not limited by "the bounds…of immediate stimuli which enslave all lower animals." We dream, we aspire, we make up stories and explanations, we wonder and we imagine; yet, Becker writes, "The world of human aspiration is largely fictitious, and if we do not understand this we understand nothing about man. It is a largely symbolic creation…." And, he continues, "The most astonishing thing of all, about man's fictions, is not that they have from prehistoric times hung like a flimsy canopy over his social world, *but that he should have come to see through himself and discover the fictional nature of his action world.*" [italics added]

In other words, humankind has learned enough, through knowledge, to recognize the gulf between myth and reality, between religious faith and scientific proof. Yet, as Wilson says, we still cling to the myth and the faith.

The conflict between folkloric and analytical learning is not new. It often manifests itself through persecuting those who dissent from accepted belief, as, respectively, the Greeks and Romans taught Socrates and the early Christians. In our tradition—our Judeo-Christian western civilization—keepers of established beliefs have long tried to stamp out those who challenged them. Dobzhansky writes:

> For 2000 years Christianity has supplied the meanings and aims at the very core of our cultural tradition. Yet, starting in the last quarter of this period, this foundation began to deteriorate, owing to its real or apparent conflicts with scientific discoveries. Literally thousands of books and articles have been written attempting to reconcile the conflicts of religion and science. When Copernicus showed that the Earth was not the center of the universe, Calvin rejected his work with the contemptuous remark: "Who will venture to place the authority of Copernicus above that of the Holy Spirit?" Later Kepler and Galileo proved that Copernicus was right, for which they were severely persecuted.

In later centuries, and continually since 1859, Darwin's theory of evolution has similarly been brushed aside by religious leaders because it contradicted the Bible. When I was three years old the world was treated to the ridiculous spectacle of the Tennessee "Monkey Trial," when William Jennings Bryan proclaimed, "It is better to trust to the rock of ages than to know the ages of rocks."

Generations after Copernicus and Galileo, the Catholic church at last accepted heliocentrism in our solar system, and more recently it has acknowledged that evolution functions the way science has proved. Yet even today many Christian leaders, some of them scientifically educated, adhere to fundamentalist creeds about the origin and nature of the universe.

The realm of science invariably contains gray areas, the spaces between what is definitively known and what we have yet to discover, explain, or understand. So scientists continually probe and poke to try to fill the gaps, generally delighting in each new discovery, whether it strengthens existing theory or challenges it.

But even such a fine mind as that of the philosopher Henri Bergson takes refuge in faith rather than pursuing the unknown with delight and scientific curiosity. His book, *Creative Evolution*, is a wonderful discourse on the vast complexities, beauty, and phenomena of the natural world, but when he confronts the chasm between what is known and the unknown, he seems to posit some "intelligent" force that resulted in the current state of the world.

Bergson's approach, it must be admitted, was widely acclaimed because it seemed to bridge the "gap" between knowledge and faith by showing that one could accept the scientific explanations of all the physical realities of the world, and still believe that they resulted from some mystical or supreme force.

But Bergson's approach, like any version of "intelligent design," effectively suggests that there's no need to continue asking questions about that gray chasm of the unknown. It suggests that the knowledge we have attained is the end of knowledge, because any explanation beyond what we know is best left to that "intelligent force" that is beyond our comprehension. It suggests, in other words, that we have reached the limits of science and must rely, from here on out, on faith.

The Sacred Narrative

It is clear from Wilson, Dobzhansky, and others that many people need a sacred narrative. They must have a sense of larger purpose, whether to explain the unknown or to maintain the "fiction of aspiration." We generally think of such a narrative, whatever its purpose and for want of a better word, as "religion."

But there should be a distinction between the terms "religion" and "worship." "Religion" generally refers to the organized faiths—Catholic, Protestant, Judaic, Islamic, etc.—and the hundreds of other structured, deistic belief systems developed over the history of civilization, and it usually involves worship of a superhuman deity or God. On the other hand "worship" does not necessitate a deity, anthropomorphic or otherwise. Worship might equally well be directed toward nature, as in various forms of pantheism, or at the pursuit of knowledge, or derived from the material history of the universe and the human species.

A non-theistic narrative is in no way debasing or uninspiring. The evolutionary epic, retold as poetry, is as intrinsically ennobling as any religious ethic. Understanding the structure of galaxies and the birth of stars is as inspiring as any creation myth; recognizing the same gene in a flatworm and an elephant should excite our hearts, minds, and "souls" in equal measure. To me, the proven material reality already discovered by science possesses more content and grandeur than all religious cosmologies combined. I find it magnificent that the development of human existence has been traced through a period of history a thousand times older than the few millennia conceived by Western religions, and that the gene pool of *Homo sapiens* is shared by, and unifies, human beings around the globe.

Why is this relevant to people of faith as well as to skeptics, to philosophers and scientists alike, and, for that matter, to all of society? The answer is simple. On the one hand, the human mind has evolved through Darwinian and/or cultural evolution to such an incredible degree that we can—*without* dependence on religion—control enough of our environment to, potentially, provide utopian conditions throughout the world. Conversely, humankind is now also capable, with weapons of mass destruction, of destroying itself and all living matter in the world because of some religious belief.

Therefore we must pose the question: is "religion" a force for good or a danger to the world?

What's Wrong With Religion?

Religion can obviously be a force for both good and ill; its value can be measured only by its results. That is where my own "ultimate concern" lies, not what happens in an afterlife, or whether there is an "intelligent designer" explaining away all the gray areas we haven't figured out yet.

I do not want to imply the nihilistic or atheistic attitude that there is nothing in which one can believe or worship. We can embrace both "religion" and specific religions so long as they uplift the human spirit, protect the vulnerable, and do not condone or encourage violation of human rights, endanger our environment, or thwart rational efforts to prevent overpopulation of the world.

But we also need to recognize that our beliefs are not, and should not be, fixed in concrete. Many millions rely on religious beliefs to explain natural or scientific phenomena; and, contrary to the beliefs of many religionists, reason and science can similarly be used to interpret historical and biblical pronouncements.

Let me again refer to E. O. Wilson's statement that religious belief—as manifested by worship—is "…the most complex and powerful force in the human mind and in all probability an ineradicable part of human nature." That assertion immediately raises the question, "Is this powerful force a genetic feature of humans, or is it something passed from parent to child in a cultural process?" In other words, is "faith" the product of nature or nurture?

Perhaps there will be some definitive evidence in the future to answer this. My firm belief is that it is largely a cultural process bolstered by incredible myths and false assumptions, based on questionable authority.

My knowledge of religion probably started with my parents. As I have noted, my father was a Congregational minister in Connecticut and later a teacher in the Vanderbilt University School of Religion. Although my parents were involved, directly or tangentially, with religious activities in my life, they never exhibited serious insistence or concern that I accept their beliefs. I wasn't indoctrinated to believe that baptism was essential; I did learn that one should only accept what was believable or logical. From the stands he took on segregation, women's rights, and other social issues, I am sure my father had a relatively liberal social outlook, but he also would have been considered an evangelist—much like Jimmy Carter. It is easy in retrospect to wonder if, in "excusing" many of his references to horrible acts in the Bible as simply allegorical exercises, I was already subject to religious "indoctrination."

Since my undergraduate major was geology, I soon began to develop another, more serious area of doubt about Christianity. Learning about the huge changes in the earth and seeing fossils left by creatures that had lived millions of years ago raised questions about the reliability and authenticity of religious documents positing that the same events took place during a span of a few thousand years—a tiny fraction of the total age of the earth. To anyone with an open mind about religion in general, this vast gulf between scientific analysis and religious interpretation of the same facts was an even greater stumbling block to religious creation stories.

As I have previously described, during my years in graduate school and my first years of professional life, my wife and I rarely went to church. Then, when the boys were about ready to start school, we began to feel their "cultural" development might be slighted by not going to church. We visited a number of denominations and, to our great joy, found the local Unitarian-Universalist church to be exactly the right combination of principles and rational beliefs among members. Fifty years later, I still share (at least provisionally) some of our UU philosophy.

Recently a number of very interesting books on religion—more specifically God—have appeared. Among them are *The End of Faith* and *Letter to a Christian Nation* by Sam Harris; Richard Dawkins's *The God Delusion*; *Breaking the Spell* and, earlier, *Darwin's Dangerous Idea,* by Daniel C. Dennett; *God is Not Great* by Christopher Hitchens; and Randall Balmer's *Thy Kingdom Come: How the Religious Right Distorts the Faith and Threatens America*. Each of these authors brings to his writing his own particular views of religious belief; they share an ability to study and analyze religion with intellectual honesty.

Harris, for example, echoes Wilson when he writes, "A kernel of truth lurks at the heart of religion, because spiritual experience, ethical behavior, and strong communities are essential for human happiness." Yet, he continues, "…our religious traditions are intellectually defunct and politically ruinous."

Dawkins, a longtime professor at Oxford University, reflecting on the 9/11 bombing of the World Trade Center and other targets, asked, "Why did these cricket-loving young men do it? Unlike their Palestinian counterparts, or their kamikaze counterparts in Japan, or their Tamil Tiger counterparts in Sri Lanka, these human bombs had no expectation that their bereaved families would be lionized, looked after or supported on martyrs' pensions. On the contrary, their relatives in some cases had to go into hiding." He concludes, "Only religious faith is a strong enough force to motivate such utter madness in otherwise sane and decent people."

Carrying that idea even further, Dennett comments that "…a toxic religious mania could end human civilization overnight. We need to understand what makes religions work, so we can protect ourselves in an informed manner from the circumstances in which religions go haywire."

A paradox of faith is that, while it's easily demonstrated that religious belief can lead to destructive, even genocidal, fanaticism—the most immoral behavior imaginable—many people, particularly those of the so-called "Religious Right," think that religion is necessary to sustain morality. But anthropological knowledge indicates that virtue and altruism were present long before religions developed. Much evidence is given in these books to show that people can be virtuous without religion and without belief in God, or any god.

How useful it would be if devoutly religious people would read them! After all, these writers are well known in philosophical circles, enjoy international recognition for their scholarship, and cite copious sources substantiating their views. Sadly, though, too many religious conservatives are so sure of their beliefs, so wedded to their unshakable faith, that they will not even read the dust covers. And, if they read some of the journalistically caustic reviews, they will likely dismiss them all as atheistic radicals—except Randall Balmer.

Balmer is an avowed Baptist evangelist, and proud of it. But he has "ratted" on his fellow evangelists by showing how they are hurting the country by trying to put their religion in the government. Separating church from state is, of course, one of the main problems associated with belief systems all over the world. To the fundamentalists' chagrin, Balmer posits that the great success of religion—particularly of the Baptists in America—has been due to, not in spite of, the separation of church and state.

There is a curious passage in Balmer's book that helps me draw a very different conclusion than Balmer does, however. He writes in his preface, "I was three or four years old when I first renounced my sins and claimed Jesus as my savior.... I revisited that moment many times through adolescence...to thereby dispel my growing intellectual and existential doubts about faith."

While Balmer views his experience as support for the power of faith through salvation, I see the opposite. In my view, no one at the age of three can know they should be "saved" without the idea having been placed in their minds by parents or other adults. Balmer's claim, therefore, provides evidence that religious faith is passed on from generation to generation by cultural means rather than genetics—by nurture, not nature.

As I noted at the beginning of this chapter, 9/11 was and remains a wake-up call for the entire world. In the years since, there have been all sorts of dire pronouncements of what caused it, of what was going to happen, and how it was a message that needed to be heeded. Almost without exception, analysts assert that religion was one, if not the only, deciding factor (up to and including Jerry Falwell's blaming it on the West's tolerance for homosexuals and atheists).

I believe the cataclysmic event teaches us another lesson. Sociology, anthropology, and paleontology have provided the knowledge that evolution, not any of the myriad creation myths, has brought people to their present form. Our intellectual understanding of our universe—our mastery of empirical truths—can explain many myths; additionally it can potentially solve social problems such as hunger, overcrowding, and illnesses that threaten all human existence.

Yet we must acknowledge that human behavior is also a product of our genetic makeup. People don't lose their instincts, hostilities, or religious and social motivations simply by gaining intellectual knowledge. We are the product of both nature and nurture, of atavistic instinct and sublime intellectual development, and we now face the dreadful possibility of the latter being placed at the service of the former. Dangerous products of our advanced intellectual accomplishment—weapons of mass destruction—could be wielded by those in the grip of our most primitive instinct—ignorant, tribal religious fanaticism.

There will be future Oklahoma City bombings and Fort Hood massacres and airline attacks, based on religion or hatred of the government or personal animosity. Perhaps our knowledge of what motivates such behavior can help us find appropriate ways to avert repetitions, just as our scientific advances can help us sustain and improve life in the future.

Imagination and "Spirit"

There is no doubt in the scientific world of the truth of the theory of evolution. But one of the quirks of the English language has decreed that the same word is used both for a provable scientific theorem and the most casual speculation. As a result, many people (some unschooled, others educated but willfully ignorant) do not accept or understand that the scientific theory is established beyond any doubt. It has withstood every challenge, every test, every skeptic's assertion that "new" evidence will disprove it. As post-Darwinian fields of inquiry have developed—carbon-14 dating; DNA sequencing; the astro- and geophysics of the K-T asteroid impact and subsequent dinosaur extinction; the discovery of a "missing link" between amphibians and mammals; even the growing evidence that birds are the descendants of dinosaurs—each has allowed new ways to test and refine Darwin's theories and find them even more firmly proven.

Many others have written at length about evolution, so for the purposes of this book I will not attempt to recap the endless proofs but simply assert that, just as we have undeniable evidence that the sun "rises" in the east, so do we have evidence that life evolves, through several processes and under a variety of stimuli and conditions, but in general from simpler to more complicated and diverse forms. (see p. 168-9 for additional discussion)

The evolution of mankind from its more primitive forebears to modern *Homo sapiens* has been, in many ways, the evolution of our imagination. The earliest creation myths and primitive religions sought explanations of whatever was inexplicable—lightning and eclipses, earthquakes and death, for example. They personified the forces that could not be seen, and they postulated magical powers and superhuman beings that wielded them. As knowledge grew of the natural world—by fits and starts and over millennia—the story-telling began to distinguish between narratives designed to explain the mysteries of the natural world from those grounded in reality—tales of hunts and ancestors and heroic feats, whether told in cave drawings in Lascaux or in epic histories recited by Greek poets.

In our heritage—indeed in most civilizations known to recorded history—these two distinct strains of story-telling have diverged, with spiritual narratives thoroughly separated from those based on reality. The "sacred" and the "profane" deal with many of the same human foibles, but in entirely different ways.

Sacred stories, ranging from creation myths to David Koresh's self-proclaimed second coming to Islamic jihad, have as their common element a firm belief in something that is not demonstrably true or, equally likely, is demonstrably *untrue*. Regardless of the evidence of the senses, the proof of testing in the laboratory and the field, the "facts on the ground," proponents of spiritual mythologies assert, often proudly and defiantly, that faith overrules fact.

The profane, or secular, imagination, however, is grounded in reality. (This is not to say that imagination does not incorporate the unreal, whether in such fantasies as wormholes in space travel or wizard children attending schools for magic. But those are subjects for a different book.) As suggested previously, the secular imagination asks *how* the world works and, when one answer is established, probes more deeply or more broadly for the next.

How is it that a rock from the ground, when heated, can exude liquid which, when cooled, turns into something else, something metallic? How is it that that metal can be reheated and shaped into strong tools? How is it that two different metals, blended, can make a new, better one? Such questions inevitably lead to probing of materials science, to molecules, atoms, protons and electrons, quarks, and ever more fundamental particles—and, of course, the invention of ever more powerful tools and instruments with which to probe them.

Or one might ask, How does an eclipse occur? How can we know where and when the sun will rise and set? What makes heavenly bodies revolve around one another? How is it that this distant galaxy seems to be moving backward through the sky? How old, how far away, how immense, is this universe? And these questions lead at last to the Big Bang theory, and the cataclysmic asteroid impact of 65.5 million years ago, and plate tectonics, and the search for "dark matter," and ever vaster interactions on the planet and in the universe.

For thousands of years of recorded history—and millennia of prehistory—human knowledge has grown as a result of the creative imagination seeking reality-based answers to such questions as these. In the process, imagination has consistently trumped the myths created by "spiritual" thinkers.

In response, those who are determined to hold fast to the "truth" of their sacred stories, against all evidence to the contrary, have repeatedly resorted to the most primitive of human characteristics—anger, fear, and violence—to challenge thinkers who would prove them wrong. As we face the possibility of additional "spiritual" reactions from fundamentalists to further progress in scientific knowledge, we must think about ways to rebut—or better, avert—them.

From my perspective, reinforcing the connections among peoples is an essential first step. We should increase humanitarian aid throughout the world. We should immediately reduce or discontinue trade with countries that do not provide basic human rights for their people. We have to try even harder to find a rational solution to the Arab-Israeli conflict, withholding financial aid if necessary as leverage. Above all, we must not allow fundamentalism, whether in Judaism, Islam, or Christianity, internationally or domestically, to continue to grow as it has in recent decades.

Chapter 10

Fundamentalism

A strict or literal interpretation of religious documents—the Bible, Koran or any other—was for centuries considered essential to maintaining established faith systems and civic order. But such unquestioning trust in their fundamental "truths" has changed in recent decades from desirable to anathema. Not only is textual literalism discredited by scholars but in fact portends hideous outcomes—*viz.*, the 9/11 and Oklahoma City bombings—if not challenged and defused. The problem is compounded because many words, phrases, or ideas derived from religious dogma, such as the "golden rule," are desirable, no matter their origin or whether one is a believer or not. Further, among believers and nonbelievers alike, much of the subject material contained in religious texts is widely accepted as simply allegorical statements of desirable principles. Hardly anyone brought up in a church-going society would dare to question this cultural indoctrination. My own life, as reflected in the thoughts and activities of my parents, was surely influenced in various ways by such mild "fundamentalism."

Recently in reading Jeff Sharlet's *The Family: The Secret Fundamentalism at the Heart of American Power,* I discovered a reference to the influence in the early twentieth century of Bruce Barton, of the prominent advertising firm Batten, Barton, Durstine & Osborn. "The Family," also called "the Fellowship," is a secretive but extensive network of adherents of a fundamentalist sect that has infiltrated corporate headquarters, many levels of American government, and even international affairs. Its central premise is that secretly amassing worldly power and wealth for its followers is the ideal way to fulfill Jesus's true teachings.

Barton's name struck a chord of memory, as I realized my father had mentioned him in various complimentary ways in my early life; he even took my mother, brother, and me to visit this man at his summer home on one of the Finger Lakes in New York. I'm not sure what his motivation was for this visit, but it surely must have been for philosophical reasons, as we drove many miles from our home in northeastern Pennsylvania to visit him.

Sharlet's reference led me to *The Man Nobody Knows*. Barton's little book, reprinted twenty-seven times between 1925 and 1927, provides an entertaining portrayal of the New Testament in 1920s business language, wherein Jesus is an extremely successful business executive. An extensive, historically informative introduction by Richard M. Fried provides essential linkage between the thoughts and attitudes that my father must have had and my own current social and political philosophy:

> Critics of *The Man Nobody Knows* made much of Barton's identity as a Madison Avenue pitchman. Barton saw no contradiction between selling soap and selling religion. To the consternation of religious conservatives, he earmarked Jesus as not only the world's greatest business leader but as its first adman too. Jesus' parables were punchy, picturesque sales appeals couched in simple language that listeners could relate to their own lives.... Jesus taught too that one must lose oneself in "service," and, said Barton, the heroes of modern business did precisely that.

Although Barton's upbringing as the son of a prominent liberal Protestant minister and his prominence as a spokesman for Madison Avenue might seem a fortuitous combination of circumstances that enabled him to tap the cultural currents of the 1920s with his book, it was not mere luck. Liberal Protestantism had abandoned harsher concepts of sin and predestination, offered a softer, gentler religion, "became assimilated to the secular creed of progress," and shifted emphasis "from shrill earnestness to formulized benevolence."

This fits what I am reasonably sure was a theme or thesis of many of my father's sermons, i.e., to allegorize the Bible in useful ways for modern times. Those sermons, my education and the subsequent development of my own thinking, and the gradual changes in theology that have reflected and paralleled the growth and development of modern societies, are all aspects of "cultural evolution," the phenomenon and the process by which people, collectively, change in reaction and response to changes in their environment. Here is how I would describe the process, or sequence:

Theology grows out of mythology. Mythology grows out of curiosity, ignorance, and fear. As our fear or ignorance (or knowledge) changes, so does our mythology, and so must the resulting theology. Thus those changes in one aspect of our knowledge or understanding lead to changes in our response to it: they *evolve*, if not in tandem then in sequence.

My father's (presumed) admiration of Barton must have dimmed in the late twenties as the Depression neared, with its obvious relevance to the Republican Party. Barton was a key adviser and close friend to Calvin Coolidge, Herbert Hoover, and Wendell Wilkie. He later was elected to Congress, "pledging to repeal one useless New Deal law each week." I assume from all that proceeded in our lives that my father—a staunch Democrat and supporter of FDR and his social reforms—would have repudiated Barton's political outlook, and hopefully his fundamentalist slant. Still I remain sadly perplexed that neither my father nor my hero Jimmy Carter ever acknowledged or spoke out about the conflict between science and theism, or challenged fundamentalists' views.

Sharlet's *The Family* has elaborated an amazing mountain of research and evidence that provides the "missing link" in explaining, for me, "the biology of ultimate concern." Given the preeminent role "religion" has achieved in the world, we must understand the calamitous nature that it can assume. Christianity, at least in the way Jesus has been depicted by the fundamentalists, and the widespread and related cultural evolution, can surely be implicated as one of the culprits.

Writing of the "Family," David Kuo, a former special assistant to the president in George W. Bush's first term, observes, "The Fellowship's reach into governments around the world is almost impossible to grasp. [The group] has… forged relationships between the U.S. government and some of the most oppressive regimes in the world, arranging prayer networks in the U.S. Congress for the likes of General Costa e Silva, dictator of Brazil; General Suharto, dictator of Indonesia; and General Park Chung Hee, dictator of South Korea."

It is difficult to estimate the number of deaths, not only military but civilian as well, that these and other dictators have caused, sometimes with our tacit approval and frequently with American weapons. An example is the treatment of East Timor by Suharto in 1975 with then-President Gerald Ford's tacit or active blessing.

The Family's activities are predominantly secret except for its "only publicized gathering…the National Prayer Breakfast, which it established in 1953 and which, with congressional sponsorship, it continues to organize at the Washington, D.C. Hilton." One has to read Sharlet's extensive documentation of the involvement of both Democrats and Republicans with Christian conservatives, such as Billy Graham, military dignitaries, and others publicly and politically religious, to appreciate the incredible degree to which tentacles of the Family extend into everyone's lives.

The Family's economic slant was, and remains, almost identical to the prewar fascism of Spain, Italy, and Germany, i.e., corporate domination of government. Though patterned after Bruce Barton's economics, I would like to believe that he could not have sanctioned in the nineteen-twenties the horrible events that would happen later.

For decades the rallying point of the Family was Communism, giving it cover for supporting the likes of Wisconsin Senator Joseph McCarthy and his blatantly un-American activities. In recent times, however, it has concentrated almost entirely on the two issues of abortion and gay rights. Its initiatives have surely influenced countless elections in recent decades, despite the group's total disregard of women's rights and scientific information about homosexuality.

One would think that fundamentalism suffered serious setbacks with the humiliating actions of Jimmy Swaggart, Billy James Hargis, Jim Bakker, Ted Haggard, and numerous other fallen evangelists. Unfortunately, as Sharlet notes, "scandal does not destroy American fundamentalism. Rather, like a natural fire that purges the forest of overgrowth, it makes the movement stronger."

In Chapter 13, "Unschooling," Sharlet exposes, with delightfully humorous sarcasm, fundamentalism's key talking points as found in many texts that are used for home schooling and in Christian academies. It is abundantly clear that fundamentalists are spreading outright contradictions of widely accepted, repeatedly verified historic, geologic, and biological realities. From my near century-long perspective it appears that fundamentalists have sweated, fretted, and allegorized so long in failed efforts to resolve the numerous contradictions of science and the Bible that they have finally given up and simply resorted to rewriting history to suit their beliefs, such as "intelligent design."

Not only do the texts falsify irrefutable records, but they appropriate attitudes and actions of historical figures as ideals to be revered by all students. Sharlet describes a hero celebrated by fundamentalist historians:

> "Stonewall Jackson of the Confederacy [was] perhaps the most brilliant general in American history and certainly the most pious. *United States History for Christian Schools* devotes more space to Jackson, "Soldier of the Cross," and the revivals he led among his troops in the midst of the Civil War, than to either Robert E. Lee or U. S. Grant.... Fundamentalists even celebrate him as an early civil rights visionary, dedicated to teaching slaves to read so that they could learn their Bible lessons."

As for literal Bible interpretation, it should be emphasized, as both Sharlet and Phillips (see p. 132) have shown, that both North and South used the Bible before, during, and after the Civil War to justify their actions.

Students should similarly learn both the good and bad about another southern icon, Andrew Jackson (no relation to Stonewall Jackon). An "anti-aristocracy" populist, he himself was a wealthy slaveowner; he believed in states rights and closed the national Bank of the United States, yet opposed states' nullification of Federal laws. He advocated a common-man's democracy, but was the author and chief proponent of the Cherokee Removal Act and the Treaty of Echota that led to the forced exile of the infamous Trail of Tears.

Perhaps, with our free speech and democratic society, we should not be concerned about religious publications and permutations of their cultural effects. But cause for alarm, as Sharlet points out, is the fact that "homeschoolers and fundamentalist academies…together account for as much as ten percent or more of the nation's children, an expanding population that buys a billion dollars' worth of educational materials annually." Also, many local school districts are dominated by fundamentalists trying to get such texts approved for *public* schools. When such important public issues as abortion, women's rights, medical research, terrorism, and the teaching of evolution are legislated by elected officials it is essential that voters—now and in the future—have the requisite understanding of historic and scientific realities to elect enlightened, honest people. But the ultimate fundamentalist objective is the very opposite of a democracy: it is the creation of a theocracy, or rule by the religious leaders in the name of their particular god.

Theocracy

A marvelous elaboration of my "missing link" in Sharlet's *The Family* is Kevin Phillips's exposé, *American Theocracy, the Peril and Politics of Radical Religion, Oil, and Borrowed Money in the 21st Century*. Strongly opposed to the religious influence over right-wing politics, Phillips (ironically, a former Republican strategist) underscores in Part II the broad influence of religion, past and present, in prominent western countries, and prophesies that, if not countered, this influence will have enormous and detrimental consequences in the coming century. He writes:

> The evangelical, fundamentalist, sectarian, and radical threads of American religion are being proclaimed openly and analyzed widely, even though bluntness is frequently muted by a pseudo-tolerance, the polite reluctance to criticize another's religion…[which] falls somewhere between unfortunate and dangerous.
>
> In contrast to the secular and often agnostic Christianity dominant in Europe, Canada, and Australia, the American view encompasses a very different outlook—one in which a large minority is in key ways closer to the intensity of seventeenth-century Puritans, Presbyterian Covenanters, and earlier Dutch or Swiss Calvinists…. The world's leading

economic and military power is also—no one can misread the data—the world's leading Bible-reading crusader state, immersed in an Old Testament of stern prophets and bloody Middle Eastern battlefields.

Phillips presents impressive data, including many citations of religious historians and prominent journalists, to show the enormous expansion of "fundamentalism" (e.g., the Southern Baptist Convention) in America, along with a corresponding decline in mainline denominations. This movement is unquestionably linked to key figures such as Billy Graham and his influence on, and the election of, many politicians, particularly presidents. Another recent book—*The Prince of War, Billy Graham's Crusade for a Wholly Christian Empire*—by Cecil Bothwell, vividly documents these presidential associations.

The history of current fundamentalist influence traces back to the Civil War. In this connection Phillips elaborates and thus demystifies several of my own lifetime contacts with modern myths. When we moved to the South during my childhood I gradually soaked up a knowledge of slavery and its residual segregation as well as the profound unfairness of it all, but as I look back I now realize that a lot of what I was hearing from the "natives" (and can still read today) was quasi-religious justification for southern intolerance: "The Civil War was not caused by slavery, but economic jealousy of the North." "Slaves were treated great—many enjoyed their life." "The Bible sanctioned slavery." And, of course, Confederate generals X, Y, and Z were "great heroes" in their devotion to biblical truths.

Having witnessed many integration measures during my lifetime, I was astonished to discover, when we moved to Clemson, SC in 1965, that the new multi-million-dollar Pickens County Courthouse, beautifully designed in colonial style, included toilets and water fountains designated "white" and "colored." One didn't have to be a rocket scientist to realize the mindset of "natives." The significance of, and the need for, the new Civil Rights Act was most apparent.

Further, my current analysis of some of what underlies present-day political opinions has been pleasantly reinforced by Phillips. The shift in southerners' allegiance from Democrat to Republican was caused, aside from outright electioneering lies ("Clinton kills babies"), by basic attitudes toward race, supported by "southern" mythology. Southern Democrats' traditional racial attitudes developed in the post-Civil War era as staunch opposition to reconstruction and integration efforts led by progressive northern Republicans. When modern Democrats (Truman, Kennedy, Johnson) advocated civil rights laws and the abolition of segregation, countless southern Democratic voters switched to the Republican party—a move that was made easier as more and more upper-middle-income and wealthy individuals could also identify with conservative Republican economic policies.

Nelson Sartoris, Professor Emeritus, Wittenberg University, has graciously allowed me to reprint below his remarks on this subject, which well represent my own analyses and Kevin Phillips's thoughts on current trends in America.

> The fundamentalist political assault on science and rationality through the substitution of faith and belief is leaving our nation impoverished and on the brink of an Age of Disenlightenment. Kevin Phillips notes that this has happened to other cultures before. As but one example he cites Rome of the fourth and fifth centuries, when the elevation of faith over logic stifled inquiry that encouraged intellectual activity, which was discredited and as a result stagnated. The libraries at Alexandria and elsewhere were closed when they embraced the dismissal of Greek logicians as set forth in the Gospel of Paul. They discarded the works of Aristotle and Ptolemy and entered the Dark Ages—and left advances in mathematics, medicine, and astronomy to Arabian culture, where it flourished until the Huns sacked Baghdad in 1395. In the religion-dominated Dark Ages in Europe there was a thousand-year gap between the last recorded astronomical observation in 475 to the publication in 1543 of Copernicus's *The Revolution of the Spheres.*
>
> Other examples that Phillips notes were in Spain, Holland, and England. Phillips postulates six characteristics of a nation past its prime. See if these apply to the current state of affairs in the U.S. The featured characteristics are:
> - widespread concern over cultural and economic decay

- growing religious fervor with an insistence on increased church-state relationship
- a rising commitment to faith as opposed to reason, along with a downplaying of science
- popular anticipation of a millennium time frame with an upcoming epochal battle, the emergence of an antichrist, an imminent second coming, and Armageddon. As Barbara Rossing has jested, "God so loved the world that he sent World War III."
- a driven national strategic and military overreach pursuing abstract international missions that the nation can't afford, economically or politically
- the withdrawal of tolerance for others by the nation's people on behalf of one true religion; Catholicism in Rome and Spain, Calvinism in Holland, Anglican Victorian values in England, and – now in the US, the growing "Onward Christian Soldiers" mentality.

Phillips suggests that we are now operating under the delusion that the U.S. is different—that our chosen exceptionalism will prevail. Will it?

The American Disenlightenment
Nelson Sartoris, unpublished remarks

I think I could turn and live with animals

I think I could turn and live with animals, they're so placid and self-contain'd...
They do not sweat and whine about their condition,
They do not lie awake in the dark and weep for their sins,
They do not make me sick discussing their duty to God,
Not one is dissatisfied, not one is demented with the mania of owning things,
Not one kneels to another, nor to his kind that lived thousands of years ago,
Not one is respectable or unhappy over the earth.

    Walt Whitman, *Leaves of Grass*, 1891 edition

Chapter 11

Summing Up a Life: Family

My life has encompassed various successful, personally rewarding, and worthwhile accomplishments in my profession and the larger society, but nothing has meant more to me than experiencing family relationships. This may sound selfish, but it is up to the reader to evaluate from the nature of events, the scope of their lives, and the presumed acceptance of concepts I may have provided, to score the record.

My father's understanding of and appreciation for the needs of the country during the Great Depression resulted in our family's participation in the early development of the TVA and Homestead projects of FDR's remarkable New Deal. It is immensely satisfying to me to have been a part of what were, perhaps, our country's greatest transformative historical events in the twentieth century. Further, his interest in and activities towards developing cooperatives were harbingers of ways to improve society. He would have been very pleased to have lived long enough to know about the huge Mondragon[35] cooperative in Spain.

Political conservatives always shout "Socialism!" whenever cooperatives are mentioned, as if it were some dirty word, in spite of the many successful cooperative enterprises like credit unions and farm and grocery co-ops. Relevant to this, in the current century, is the success of the Bank of North Dakota[36], the only state bank in the nation, which has been in existence since 1919 and a striking contrast to other financial institutions during the recent overwhelming banking crisis.

As for my nuclear family, it was my everlasting good fortune to have met Ruth in college, and to have had her as the mother of our family and constant inspiration for whatever successes I may ever be credited. The accomplishments of our children and grandchildren—creativity and self-reliance as well as graduate degrees, publications, inventions, and awards—would not have been possible without her.

Whether or not my feelings or opinions had any influence on their various choices, it is of considerable satisfaction that each of my sons independently chose different disciplines, professions, or specialties in their successful lives. I believe that the greatest asset in life is the exercise of imagination and/or creativity and that both are building blocks to happiness and success, beliefs reinforced by my sons' careers:

Alan is a professional in anthropology and archaeology, Steven a horticulturalist and landscape designer; David entered government service in city and regional planning, Michael chose materials science as a ceramics engineer, and Jeffrey opted for public outreach through media production. What father wouldn't be proud of such sons?

I was also fortunate to have parents who were open-minded about most matters of life. While I am critical of their theism, I recognize they were firmly in the grip of their own cultural evolution: their lives and thus their philosophy were governed by Christian traditions, beliefs, and literal words of the Bible that were in use for hundreds of years before them. And though they were well-read and educated as to the theories of Copernicus, Sir Francis Bacon, and Darwin, they were not unlike most people of their generation who did not comprehend the ultimate implications of these historical thinkers and their ideas, or the directions in which such discoveries must ultimately lead—nor were they willing to stray from their strict fundamentalist ideas based in the Bible. Even now apologists for the Bible, including both highly educated theologians and a sprinkling of scientists, claim that its stories are simply allegories for actual steps in *creation* and formulae for living. Had my parents had the benefit of later scientific discoveries, both real and philosophical, perhaps I would have no reason to be critical. Their example provided me with an indelible prototype of an ideal for people motivated, in part, by faith, thus making it difficult for me to imagine how the ultimate realities of their lives would have been improved with greater knowledge.

Though most religions have brought about improvements, to some degree, in adherents' welfare or general humanitarian progress, they have offset those benefits in a decidedly negative way through the countless wars and persecutions they have undertaken. And while vast numbers of people have successfully turned to institutionalized religion for emotional or "spiritual" comfort, inspiration, and guidance toward ethical living, I hope that this memoir will suggest values for even greater reward in one's personal life, and possibilities for a utopian world, without the negative aspects of theistic religions.

Souls

In the usual conventional sense or dictionary definition, the soul is considered the spiritual or immaterial part of a human being, the attribute that shapes a person's moral or emotional nature or sense of identity. Since this is a rather vague or esoteric description, I have developed my own understanding of soul (p. xii). For this discussion, I use the word primarily for generalizing the difference between animals and plants, i.e., non-thinking organisms.

The word itself is a mental construct based on such other constructs as "spirituality" and "heaven" and "God," largely religious in content, which can be conceptualized only by mental imagery—imagination—that itself is based on information from society's narrative (told by parents or elders, shown in pictures, or described in stories, and deduced therefrom). For many, probably most, people, even well-educated ones, this "soul" concept is central to their religious attitudes or notion of God.

An incident in my doctor's office illustrates my point. During the interminable waits between phases of my examination, the doctor noticed a little book I was reading—*The Souls of Animals,* by Gary Kowalski—and seemed interested. After a while I had the temerity to ask, "Do you think animals have souls?"

After he left the room for a while and then returned, he replied, "No, I don't think they have souls, because they cannot go to heaven."

I was quite taken aback and replied, "Well I seriously doubt if there is a heaven, but if there is one, my dog Lucas can surely go with me."

Even this doctor, whose medical training necessarily included extensive familiarity with the scientific method, relied on such a vague construct as "heaven" despite a complete lack of evidence for an afterlife. Nothing supports the existence of an afterlife or a heaven, other than anecdotes which are, by their very nature, not susceptible to verification or testing required by science and can, therefore, be accepted only by "faith." For some, faith in things "spiritual" moves them to ignore their training, knowledge, and reason in order to hold such ideas; for anyone who prefers evidence, such ideas are unbelievable.

Kowalski provides convincing evidence, on the other hand, of mental activity for many species of animals, evidence (and intelligence) that is generally unknown or misunderstood by most people. Much scientific work has confirmed empirically (though not necessarily *explained*) demonstrations of communication and related behavior among animals—humans included. He writes:

> They have emotional lives, experience love and fear, and possess their own integrity, which suffers when not respected. They play and are curious about their world. They develop loyalties and display altruism…. Like most dog lovers Darwin was convinced that "man's best friend" possesses something closely resembling a conscience. There can, I think, be no doubt that a dog feels shame, as distinct from fear, and something like modesty when begging too often for food.

From this brief account, my own concept of the human soul may be inferred. It is a (or the) central, animating part of consciousness, of our selves and our kinships. (It might also be noted here that the root of "animating" is the Latin "anima," meaning "soul" or "spirit.")

Belief

Our families and friends—and some strangers—along with their accomplishments, occupy most of the stage in the drama of our existence. Still, there is a part that relates to nature; though usually relatively small, it can in some cases (such as Thoreau's) occupy essentially all of one's life in philosophic naturalism. While I have great interest in the beauty, inner details of structure, physiology, and the vast array of uses of plants, I have no interest in anthropomorphism. Early in graduate school I learned that plants do not bend upwards because they are "seeking the light" nor downward to "seek water." There is no "mind" guiding their activities. These phenomena are actually caused by auxins (extractable chemical compounds) that cause cells to elongate. Since specific auxins respond to gravity and to sunlight, the cells on whichever side is necessary for growth, upward or downward, are those that respond to those stimuli. This simplification is included merely to demonstrate that science can explain many mysteries of life without relegating all unknowns to "God."

Animal life (humans included) introduces an entirely unique universe. With reflective brains, possibilities emerge for interactions with other creatures. We lack, at this time, a complete understanding of *how* and *why* we think as we do, but in recent years there have been huge scientific advances in understanding the neural, chemical, structural, and behavioral relationships of the brain. As science continues to explain critical features in the biology of our behavior, it seems only reasonable to put such findings to use in our philosophical constructs, and seek solutions to all sorts of questions of why and how we exist and behave as we do. Darwin's writings provide the most profound example.

Freud's and Jung's observations, presumably pivotal in behavioral science, led me to make my own, similarly crude, hypothetical conceptual theory, particularly with respect to explaining cultural evolution—since it has had such disastrous repercussions in history. It goes like this: in the evolution of humans, the mind (brain) has developed into a prodigious organ for *storing* information. Along with this came the ability to *imagine*, that is, interrelate bits of stored information to devise an explanation of a problem or a solution to some need. From this, my concept of steps in an individual's cultural indoctrination develops as follows:

1. When a child is born its brain accepts sensory information from what is felt, seen, or actually perceived by experimentation, and it gradually builds a database for relating *realities*, e.g., fire is hot and will burn your fingers.
2. Much of this type of information has been received from the mother, which verifies its validity.
3. Along with this the child (often) receives the mother's (or another's) words about imaginary *spiritual* thoughts or vague concepts of God and/or religion.
4. The child has no way of discriminating between factual and imaginary information.
5. After various periods of continual repetition, these concepts recede into (and take root in) the mental depths of *known* or established fact.

Examples of this progression became vivid for me through two works of poetry. The first is the frequently cited children's bedtime prayer, "Now I lay me down to sleep." My mother never suggested that I recite it, but she had no objection or, at least, no comment, when I did so from time to time. Where did I learn it? I probably picked it up from hearing it repeated by other children, and considered kneeling and praying appropriate for a pre-bedtime exercise. But I hardly understood the meaning:

>Now I lay me down to sleep
>I pray the Lord my soul to keep.
>If I should die before I wake,
>I pray the Lord my soul to take.

How is a child of three or four to know what the "soul" is? And why, at that age, should he start questioning (or fearing) what may happen when he dies? Nevertheless, these subconscious thoughts pervade one's mind for many years and are relevant to one's attitude about the possibility—or impossibility—of God.

The second item is the Twenty-third Psalm, which I learned, of course, in the King James Version. It is certainly a beautiful and inspirational piece. But for a small child hearing it repeatedly from preschool up to some level of rational understanding, the psalm carries numerous abstract implications—allegorical, to be sure, but subject to adult explanations—that can lead to unnecessary fears or misunderstandings of some potential "Lord" or "God": "green pastures," "quiet waters," "shadow of death," "mine enemies," "the house of the LORD"? One could comment on the "Lord's Prayer" (see p. 8) with similar ideas, and it is small wonder—and of great importance—that it is considered improper, or at least inappropriate, to be recited in institutions protected by Constitutional separation of church and state.

These religio-cultural influences prevail from generation to generation. Such "knowledge" with no empirical basis can, of course, sometimes be modified by actual discoveries or scientific experimentation. Sadly, though, human frailty persistently allows *imaginary* information to deny, or at least discredit, *known realities* such as the age of the Earth, the size of the universe, the date life originated, and other significant, scientific discoveries.

The ability to *imagine*—to relate different bits of mental information to make a plan or hypothesis to be experimentally tested—is, of course, a great asset. Without this intellectual attribute our modern lifestyle would never have been possible. Still, without experimental verification, and in face of the ease with which <u>mis</u>information can be distributed (magazines, books, tracts, television, radio, the Internet, and now iPads, -Pods, and -Phones), human imagination can also be detrimental to knowledge, as, for example, in fundamentalists' determined denial of evolution and misunderstanding of *creation*.

Religious belief systems (or cultural "philosophies") are largely based on untestable, imaginary assumptions. Typical is the double-negative presumption: "Since you cannot *prove* there is <u>no</u> God, then it *logically* could be possible." This irrational "logic" is widespread among

> The Twenty-third Psalm
> The LORD is my shepherd; I shall not want. He maketh me to lie down in green pastures: he leadeth me beside the still waters. He restoreth my soul: he leadeth me in the paths of righteousness for his name's sake. Yea, though I walk through the valley of the shadow of death, I will fear no evil: for thou art with me; thy rod and thy staff they comfort me. Thou preparest a table before me in the presence of mine enemies: thou anointest my head with oil; my cup runneth over. Surely goodness and mercy shall follow me all the days of my life: and I will dwell in the house of the LORD for ever.
> *The Book of Common Prayer*
> The Church of England, 1662

established religions, no matter how irreconcilable the differences among them or, for that matter, within the dogma of just one religion—Christianity.

But in the case of Humanism (or Naturalism), there is no such deity to disprove, nor are there such irreconcilable inconsistencies and logical fallacies. This is not to say Humanism has no beliefs, only that it rejects unfounded or untestable ones. Also, in place of creeds or dogma, which are the essence of other religions, Humanism offers principles of behavior [see sidebar] that encompass or subsume the *virtues* of widely established religions—in essence, the "golden rule." In contrast to the dominant theisms that have existed for centuries, Humanism represents a promising pinnacle of philosophical understanding in the period of cultural evolution to which I have been exposed.[37]

What then, is the answer to the favorite question of theists: "What gives you hope, and how can you exist, without God?" (i.e., "without the imaginary spiritual guidance of some supernatural being?")? The answer is embodied in words of many revered humanist figures, both present and past. The editors of *Imagine There's No Heaven: Voices of Secular Humanism*[38] offer this list:

Secular Humanism Is...

This list is adapted from one written by Paul Kurtz, which often appears in *Free Inquiry*, the magazine published by The Council for Secular Humanism.

"*We are*:
- concerned with securing justice and fairness in society and with eliminating discrimination and intolerance,
- committed to the application of reason and science to the understanding of the universe and to the solving of human problems,
- deeply concerned with the moral education of our children, in order to nourish reason and compassion,
- engaged by the arts no less than the sciences,
- citizens of the universe and are excited by discoveries still to be made in the cosmos,
- skeptical of untested claims to knowledge, open to novel ideas, and welcoming of new departures in our thinking.

We believe:
- in the cultivation of moral excellence,
- in the common moral decencies of altruism, integrity, honesty, truthfulness, responsibility. [However, Humanist ethics is amenable to critical, rational guidance; there are normative standards that we discover together. Moral principles are tested by their consequences.]
- in an open and pluralistic society and that democracy is the best guarantee of protecting human rights from authoritarian elites and repressive majorities.
- that scientific discovery and technology can contribute to the betterment of life.
- in enjoying life here and now and in developing our creative talents to their fullest,
- in optimism rather than pessimism, hope

~ continued ~

"Great humanists and free thinkers of the past include philosophers from Socrates and Epicurus to Bertrand Russell and Albert Camus, writers and poets such as Percy Bysshe Shelly and Marian Evans (George Eliot), scientists such as Charles Darwin and Albert Einstein, social activists such as Elizabeth Cady Stanton and Andrei Sakahrov, and political leaders such as Thomas Jefferson and Pandit Jawaharlal Nehru."

My own answer is this: Humanism may be characterized by the inspiration and beauties of art, music, theater and literature; the creativity and awe of architecture, modern inventions and institutions; the grandeur of nature, which encompasses incredible vistas of our earth and other planets and the galaxies of the magnificent universe of which it is a part; the incredible variety of plant and animal life, and even greater knowledge of their invisible aspects, i.e., the genetics, chemistry, and physics of their internal processes; and above all the joy of helping people and animals be happy, live better, and be able to have a good and sustainable environment. Utilizing, enjoying, and participating in these elements are not only sufficient for an ideal existence, but also do not depend on belief in—

---

rather than despair, learning in the place of dogma, truth instead of ignorance, joy rather than guilt or sin, tolerance in place of fear, love instead of hatred, compassion over selfishness, beauty instead of ugliness, and reason rather than blind faith or irrationality,

- in supporting the disadvantaged and handicapped so that they will be able to help themselves,

- in the fullest realization of the best and noblest that we are capable of as human beings.

We deplore efforts to denigrate human intelligence, to seek to explain the world in supernatural terms, and to look outside nature for salvation.

We are committed to the principle of the separation of church and state.

We cultivate the arts of negotiation and compromise as a means of resolving differences and achieving mutual understanding.

We respect the right to privacy. Mature adults should be allowed to fulfill their aspirations, to express their sexual preferences, to exercise reproductive freedom, to have access to comprehensive and informed health care, and to die with dignity.

We attempt to transcend divisive parochial loyalties based on race, religion, gender, nationality, creed, class, sexual orientation, or ethnicity, and strive to work together for the common good of humanity.

We want to protect and enhance the earth, to preserve it for future generations, and to avoid inflicting needless suffering on other species.

We affirm humanism as a realistic alternative to theologies of despair and ideologies of violence and as a source of rich personal significance and genuine satisfaction in the service to others."

or invocation to—a supernatural deity.

Several years back I expressed my beliefs in verse and set them to music (see Appendix B). The text is below.

Reality Moves On

The record, speed and nature of the world are now well known;
From astronomy and then geology the seeds were sown;
Truth from physics, math, and chemistry for everyone is shown:
    Reality moves on.

Our wealth of knowledge of the world continues to expand;
It is based upon the facts of science we can understand;
Carbon dated fossils show what lived all over our great land:
    Reality moves on.

Anthropology reveals how instinctive drives evolve;
Love, hate, fear and altruism help in forming our resolve;
To make a world where human conflicts in the world dissolve:
    Reality moves on.

Our ancestors' ancient myths and fears are mostly now extinct;
Neuroscience has now shown how and why we behave and think;
Imagination, creativity provide the link:
    Reality moves on.

Solving mysteries of DNA and human genome;
Are feats that show the mind of science not asleep at home;
Ventures to unknown space by courageous thoughts and deeds have shown:
    Reality moves on.

Human minds have brought great joy and helped our lives today;
Music, art and science written down by hand or other way;
Continue making progress toward utopia some day:
    Reality moves on.

                                        Joseph Haun 02/08/2007

Reality

Another favorite question from theists is, "How, then, do you account for *creation*?" In my lifetime the answers have emerged (for me and hopefully others) from actually experiencing realities as well as reading history and the findings of scientists.

Before elaborating on this, I should emphasize that a true scientist would be arrogant—and impolite as well—not to acknowledge the agnostic possibility that some theistic or "supernatural" origin of life will still be discovered in the future. We must remember that what was "supernatural" to our forebears entered the realm of "natural" as soon as—but only when—we could explain it scientifically. "Dark matter" and "dark energy" still elude us, because we have yet to figure them out or discover enough about them to make the postulation work scientifically; but someday perhaps we will—or conversely the theory will have to be revised out of existence. Perhaps, then, some entity outside our known rules of existence will also be discovered and explained some day, the result of greater knowledge elucidated by a realm of science as unthought of today as telecommunication via the radio spectrum and satellite transmission was a thousand years ago.

However, it is also willful ignorance to deny logical explanations that are based on valid and repeated experimental evidence and provide appropriate linkage with *theories*. Within just one area of science—geology—there are many profound and testable realities about the age of the earth, its possible origin, etc., bolstered by the relatively recent use of radiocarbon dating, that should disprove biblical literalists as well as the allegorists who seek to find spiritual truth in much of the religious doctrine of our time. With such an analysis of scientists' work also comes a wealth of background on their personal lives, what has shaped their lives and opinions on *philosophical* matters. Therefore, despite prevailing attitudes about the existence of god(s)—beliefs that have provided humans over centuries so much comfort, many of them demonstrably impossible—one should realize that strong evidence exists for plausible explanation of creation within current, even if incomplete, understandings of physical and spatial realities of space and time, cf. Einstein's Theory of Relativity[39] ($E=mc^2$) and this evidence stands without any reliance on divine intervention.

As my friend Nelson Sartoris writes:

"In the first fraction of a second (thought to be about 10^{-43} sec) after the Big Bang, it was so hot that atoms not only didn't exist yet, but that the components of atoms (neutrons, electrons, protons, etc) also didn't exist yet. In *a few fractions of a second* afterwards, the universe had "cooled" sufficiently that elementary particles that atoms are composed of started to form. These were quarks, electrons, neutrinos, etc. After a few seconds, "cooling" to about 3,000 billion degrees Kelvin occurred, enough to allow the formation of protons and neutrons, called hadron particles, out of this "quark" soup. After about a minute of additional cooling these naked nuclei (it was still much too hot for electrons to be captured by these nuclei to form real atoms) began to fuse with each other to form other nuclei such as deuterium (an isotope of hydrogen that contains one proton and one neutron), tritium (another isotope of hydrogen containing one proton and two neutrons), and helium (two protons and two neutrons).

It would take another 200,000-300,000 years before the universe cooled enough to permit these raw nuclei to capture and retain electrons. One can say the first true atoms, with both a nucleus and electrons, occurred at this time. The appearance of the rest of the known atoms would have to wait until star formation occurred, which would transform this hydrogen and helium into other elements (Li, C, etc.) through the process of fusion occurring in our sun today. It would take longer for heavy elements to be created in the supernova explosions of large stars.

After atoms had been created, it was only a matter of time and sufficient cooling for the inevitable creation of the first simple molecules. Most likely the first molecule was H_2, formed by the reaction of two hydrogen atoms. Then other simple molecules, such as CH_4, NH_3, and H_2O, would inevitably form, dictated by the simple rules of chemical bonding of atoms.

More complex molecules, in particular simple amino acids and nucleic acids, which are the building blocks for amino acids and DNA, inevitably followed. This early synthesis of the building blocks of life was beautifully demonstrated by Urey and Miller in 1953 at the University of Chicago when they took a mixture of the gases that constituted the early atmosphere of Earth, CH_4, NH_3, H_2O, and H_2, and energized them with an electrical discharge, simulating lightning. In the resultant soup they found molecules of amino acids and the nucleotide bases of DNA."

Urey's and Miller's experiments were designed to test an existing scientific theory to see if the ideas postulated could be supported by evidence. They were. The results can be repeated by other scientists in other labs; hence the experiments were successful, and the theory—to the extent it was tested—is validated. What is more believable: such verifiable tests, or myths that ignore them?

The Internet site www.thinkquest.org provides related information in easily accessible language.

Simple Biological Molecules Were Formed Under Prebiotic Conditions

During the first billion years on earth, there was little free oxygen and no ozone to absorb UV [ultraviolet] radiation from the sun. Yet, simple organic molecules were formed under such harsh conditions. Laboratory experiments simulating the primitive earth have confirmed that organic molecules could have been formed. When gases such as CO_2, CH_4, NH_3, and H_2 were heated with water and energized by electrical discharge or by UV radiation, they reacted and formed small organic molecules. More importantly, the organic molecules that were crucial to life (amino acids, nucleotides, sugars, and fatty acids) were also generated.

library.thinkquest.org/C004535/on_the_origin_of_cells.html
(accessed 9/25/11)

In a feature for *Discover* magazine author Boonsri Dickinson puts the building blocks of science in the language of religion.

#98: First Molecule of Life Discovered?

In the beginning there was RNA. RNA begat DNA, and

DNA begat lipids, carbohydrates, and proteins: That is Genesis according to the "RNA world" hypothesis, a leading but still sketchy picture of how life began. In June, chemist Reza Ghadiri of the Scripps Research Institute started filling in details.

Ghadiri posited the existence of a helper molecule: a kind of prebiotic template that might have enabled RNA to spawn more complex organic compounds. Then he actually constructed a version of the molecule in his lab. Called tPNA (thioester peptide nucleic acid), it comprises the same four base pairs as DNA. The amazing thing about tPNA is that it adapts, chameleon-like, as it interacts with other molecules. When Ghadiri poured tPNA molecules into a soup of DNA bits, the tPNA base pairs reshuffled until they matched the sequence of a DNA strand. When he mixed tPNA with a single strand of RNA, it conformed to RNA's structure. And when he let tPNA mingle with its own kind, the molecules danced until their structures became stable. In short, Ghadiri says, it "exhibits the most basic properties needed for evolution."

The next challenge for Ghadiri is to show that tPNA can self-replicate, crucial for a DNA precursor. If so, an RNA world—and the whole field of biogenesis—will look a lot more credible.

www.discovermagazine.com/2010/jan-feb/098/article_print
(accessed 9/25/11)

Creativity

My life story is not put forth as a paragon of creativity, despite the fact that, at a number of points, there have been bursts of personal discovery that were certainly satisfying. Creativity is not necessarily doing something entirely new in the world, but it delivers essentially the same pleasure, through the discovery that you yourself can actually do or create something that you previously could not. Curiosity could be said to impel a discovery, but more often necessity—as the old adage goes—is the mother of invention. Certainly this was the case with the three houses we built. Our needs and desires, with a growing family, were far beyond our budget. Doing something with no formal training beyond casual observation can certainly be rewarding, both personally satisfying and economically helpful.

Each of the entirely different professional positions in which I have been involved was basically dependent on the discovery and/or development of something new, and three of the five were, fortunately, highly successful. Many minor, totally obscure (unpublished) discoveries were made in trying to find, or set up, ways to reach a given objective, such as a chemical to kill one kind of weed but not the crop plants among which it was grown, or finding suitable geographic sites for potentially new crops—and all cultural requirements—for species with promising chemical constituents but never grown commercially. An idea was distilled from years of New Crop research in the USDA, and elaborated at Clemson, for quantifying plant development which resulted in the *Haun scale,* analogous to other measurement units such as *watts, volts,* and *amperes* as measurements of electricity. The idea was not totally original, but shared with J. J. Higgins, as he had utilized the principle on garden peas. It was given the name *Haun scale* by some other research personnel because of wide acceptance in research on wheat and other cereals on which my work at Clemson was centered.

The work I undertook, both professionally and in private life, was, at heart, the result of imagination: the creative impulse harnessed by a thirst for knowledge and a curiosity about the world. It was creativity grounded in reality, and the results were believable, whether tangible—houses built and plants grown and children reared to adulthood—or confined to the realm of new scientific knowledge, insights, and ideas. The unbelievable constructs of faith—such imaginary places as heaven and hell, or the guidance of a supernatural, divine hand watching over me—cannot compare to such achievements.

Invictus

Out of the night that covers me,
Black as the Pit from pole to pole,
I thank whatever gods may be
For my unconquerable soul.

In the fell clutch of circumstance
I have not winced nor cried aloud.
Under the bludgeonings of chance
My head is bloody, but unbowed.

Beyond this place of wrath and tears
Looms but the Horror of the shade,
And yet the menace of the years
Finds, and shall find, me unafraid.

It matters not how strait the gate,
How charged with punishments the scroll.
I am the master of my fate:
I am the captain of my soul.

William Ernest Henley (1849-1930)

Chapter 12

Making Life Worthwhile

The crucial element in undertaking creative endeavors is determination, or as Edison said, perspiration—not necessarily physical sweat (though that is probably a healthful part of the process), but the perspiration of continuing in face of obstacles. "Invictus" by William Ernest Henley, which I learned at a young age and still appreciate, has been an inspiration for my own work, values, and beliefs throughout my life.

As I look back over my life—a substantial part of a century—I realize that from my knowledge (admittedly naive) a perspective that can be useful has emerged. Though my references are sparse, those noted in the bibliography will suffice for recommendations to readers. And the references within my references fan out to such a wide array of thinkers, explorers, and historians as to make sure my hypotheses have a sufficiently broad base of support. I hope that this work will serve as a synthesis of others' views as well as my own. I will try to focus on the problems of humankind and the world as if approaching from outer space in some sort of sci-fi vehicle.

As you would imagine, the landing point will be at random, my view on arrival may be biased. However, it will have been preceded by several revolutions of the earth, plus *Superman's* inside knowledge of geology, anthropology, biology, sociology, history, and all the rest of human studies (i.e., everything covered in Will & Ariel Durant's eleven-volume *The Story of Civilization*). Furthermore, it should not take a rocket scientist to make a few basic suggestions (not, of course, in order of "importance," for they could be reordered in various ways with equal profundity).

Above all, everything people do is qualified by pursuing the necessities of life—food, clothing, shelter, and the needs of the family, i.e. survival. So it is rather trite to suggest all sorts of steps for improving society until one has solved "first" problems first. I was through college and beginning to start a family before giving much serious thought to societal improvements—and even then had no spare time or money to make a start. Hopefully everyone will find a rewarding, pleasant, even socially beneficial, means of earning a living. Sadly, the residual excesses of the Industrial Revolution have not been erased. Vast numbers of people toil under distressing conditions to make a living. Therefore, these suggestions are purposely directed to those who have found space in their lives, no matter how grueling their toil, to think about the plight of *others*, their relatives and descendants, and certainly to those who have come to retirement and wonder, or are perplexed, about what they should do.

First—Perfect Democracy

Throughout the history of humankind, conflicts over land, religion, and modes of living have given way to predicaments such as those we face today. Democracy is great, but ours is by no means perfect. While it pretends to provide *life, liberty, the pursuit of happiness* along with *justice for all*, there are many things that can be improved.

Begin with the most basic feature of a democracy—VOTE. Obviously, a system intended to represent all the people assumes that all the people will vote. Yet the percentage of people voting in most of our elections is distressingly low. However, to be able to vote intelligently one must read or listen to adequate sources of information—a task that, of course, most people don't take the time to pursue.

Next—PARTICIPATE. Go to precinct meetings, volunteer to help with related activities. Participate in voter registration drives. Write letters to editors, support favorite candidates, give money to worthwhile causes. Read, keep up with current events, seek out *issues* that need attention, organize or join groups to correct injustices and help those who are underprivileged by existing conditions. Inform your candidates and elected officials of your interests and ideas for improving life for everyone. An issue to which I have given attention for the last decade is money in politics and the degree to which it has altered justice in our country. One satisfying result, due to efforts of North Carolina Voters for Clean Elections, has been the law for financing election of the state's Supreme Court and Appellate Court judges with public funds.

To elaborate on this issue, consider the fact that in most of our nation the judges—who decide on *justice* for everyone—are *elected*. It usually costs a lot of money to run a campaign, travel, give speeches, hire staff, and do everything necessary to get elected. Who are the first individuals who will give money to help elect judges favorable to their interests? Trial lawyers, of course, who will likely appear in their courts defending their clients—frequently great corporations. Then imagine how the subsequently elected judge will react when deciding an issue affecting some poor individuals, in a remote area, not well known or understood by the general public (or even present, let alone represented by a lawyer), but of great financial concern to the corporate client. Test your imagination further and realize that the lawyer's income for the future will be determined by his potential bias in the issues at hand. Thus, our justice system, like all other aspects of our government managed by elected officials, is subject to the influence of money (see pp. 108-110).

Beware the Fervor of Religion

As I have acknowledged, history is replete with examples of beneficial, compassionate, comforting—even exciting—practices of organized religions. Unfortunately, in the vast majority of cases, their presumed role in helping disadvantaged people is minor compared with their major efforts erecting buildings, hiring leaders, and promoting questionable dogma. One can heartily support efforts such as the American Friends Service Committee or the Unitarian-

Universalist Service Committee. In addition to my support of these is an inclination toward The Ethical Culture Society and other organizations described later, for supporting my humanist philosophy; the protection and enjoyment of nature, as shown on the cover of this book; and the happiness of people through the organizations I am helping support. Such practices as meditation (c.f. Buddhism) can also be most enjoyable and beneficial to an individual, though this is, to me, less an "organized religion" than a personal practice, which can be done most efficaciously in private.

It has been theorized by anthropologists that religions may have originated in primitive societies as dancing and singing rituals to enhance their enjoyment, as well as the quality and safety of their lives. Their guides, shamans or "witch-doctors," prescribed procedures for ensuring successful crop production and protection from all sorts of environmental hazards such as lightning. Fears of terrifying unknown dangers, especially fears of the afterlife, were exacerbated, and solutions were developed using rituals, prayers, and other religious rites.

Current religions doubtless morphed from these early primitive societies. As scientific discoveries have unfolded to explain and protect us from the vicissitudes of nature, our dependence on, and belief in, religious pronouncements has gradually waned; sadly, too many practices, beliefs, and creeds remain, in the face of clear and repeatedly demonstrated proof that they are impossible. Moreover, many are unjust, and prevent the advance of human freedom and social democracy. Women and girls, whose rights have improved somewhat in the last century, still suffer terrible indignities, such as infant mutilation, child marriage, restrictions on birth control, and limited or no access to abortion—even in cases of rape and incest. For centuries (since Copernicus) the Catholic church, in the name of Christianity, has been the chief proponent of these attitudes; but many other denominations, especially Christian fundamentalism, Orthodox Judaism, and Islam, also adhere to them.

In many current religious circles "proof" of existence of a supernatural deity is based in the absolute (or allegorical) inerrancy of the Bible. Their "reasoning" is as follows: the Bible is the word of God, and every word in it, being His, must be true, and therefore proves his existence, for there would be no Bible without God. Such reasoning, of course, is completely circular, each premise resting on the next, and none of them based on evidence or subject to proof; an endless syllogism with no facts but numerous faith-based assertions.

For many—particularly Christian fundamentalists—additional "proof" relies on scientists' alleged *inability* to prove the scientific validity of evolution: "You can't watch evolution happening, so you simply trust Darwin's words that it is. You take Darwin's word over God's." In short, the anti-evolutionists create a false equivalency, claiming that on "both sides of the argument," proof relies on faith, and faith is the only proof required. And because God is greater than Darwin, clearly He wins.

But real proofs of evolution are rampant. As J. A. Coyne points out in his book, *Why Evolution Is True*, Darwinian theory is supported with ample, not to say overwhelming, evidence. The theory of evolution—and yes, it is a *scientific theory*, which means an explanation subject to prediction and testing, i.e., that fits all the known facts and is subject to testing and analysis by the scientific method, and that can be refined and strengthened when new facts are discovered—comprises both the origin and the evolution of species. Its six features are *evolution* (genetic identity changes over time); *gradualism* (change occurs over many generations); *speciation* (change leads to different species that cannot, by definition, reproduce together); *common ancestry* (the flip side of speciation, i.e., where species came from as opposed to where they ended up); *natural selection* (the commonly referred to "survival of the fittest," or those best adapted to specific conditions); and *nonselective mechanisms* of evolutionary change (the rare, but naturally occurring, mutations and deteriorations in genetic sequences that sometimes lead to non-adaptive change).

Each of these six features has been tested using a variety of methods ranging from carbon-dating to DNA analysis. For one-and-a-half centuries, predictions based on Darwinian theory have been made about what must be true, and each time new evidence—such as new kinds of fossils—surfaces, it has been proven to support the predictions of Darwin's theory. Since 1859, no person and no scientific test has been able to refute Darwin.

One of the most astounding proofs was a "missing link" between fish and mammals. Scientists had long predicted, based on shared DNA, common features, and gradualism (as well as geological evolution resulting from plate tectonics), that in the late Devonian there should have been an animal exhibiting features of both fish and early mammals. Knowing that an area of Canada had 400-million-year-old rocks that had not been melted and transformed by subduction, University of Chicago paleontologist Neil Shubin and a colleague went there in 2004 to look for it. As BBC News science reporter Rebecca Morelle wrote in 2006:

> [*Tiktaalik roseae*] shares some characteristics with a fish; it has fins with webbing, and scales on its back. But it also has many features in common with land animals. It has a flat crocodile-like head with eyes positioned on top and the beginnings of a neck—something not seen in fish.
>
> "When we look inside the fin, we see a shoulder, we see an elbow, and we see an early version of a wrist, which is very similar to that of all animals that also walk on land," said Professor Shubin.
> http://news.bbc.co.uk/2/hi/4879672.stm
> (accessed 9/25/11)

Perhaps the most outlandish and perplexing aspect of religion in our time is the insistence of evangelists and fundamentalists on the inerrant validity of the Bible. My father, Charles Haun, as recounted earlier, was also guilty of this affront to knowledge and facts, though, in fairness, he was surely the product of cultural evolution from his parents. Further, his support of inerrancy was generally—and mercifully—restricted to the New Testament, in his efforts to allegorically demonstrate its relevance to modern times. Some years ago, in response to those preachers, ministers, pastors, and priests who take the entire Bible as an absolute guide to living, Dr. James M. Kauffman, a prominent specialist in Special Education at the University of Virginia, sent a humorous but accurate posting to Dr. Laura Schlesinger's radio show. The posting "went viral," shooting around the Internet for several years, and it's still worth reading if only for the reminder of the complete lack of consistency among those who claim to be absolutist about inerrancy.

> "Dear Dr. Laura:
>
> Thank you for doing so much to educate people regarding God's Law.... When someone tries to defend the homosexual life style, for example, I simply remind them that Leviticus 18:22 clearly states it to be an abomination.... End of the debate.

I do need some advice from you, however on some other elements of God's Laws and how to follow them.

- Leviticus 25:44 states that I may possess slaves, both male and female, providing they are purchased from neighboring nations. A friend of mine claims this applies to Mexicans, but not Canadians. Can you clarify? Why can't I own Canadians?

- I would like to sell my daughter into slavery, as sanctioned in Exodus 21:7. In this day and age, what do you think would be a fair price for her?

- I have a neighbor who insists on working on the Sabbath. Exodus 35:2 clearly states he should be put to death. Am I morally obligated to kill him myself, or should I ask the police to do it?

- I know from Leviticus 11:8 that touching the skin of a dead pig makes me unclean, but may I still play football if I wear gloves?

- My uncle has a farm. He violates Leviticus 19:19 by planting two different crops in the same field, as does his wife by wearing garments made of two different kinds of thread (cotton/polyester blend). He also tends to curse and blaspheme a lot. Is it really necessary that we go to all the trouble of getting the whole town together to stone them? Lev. 24:10-16. Couldn't we just burn them to death in a private affair, like we do with people who sleep with their in-laws? Lev. 20:14...."

Despite the narrow focus and bogus doctrines of many churches, it is still exhilarating to occasionally visit elaborate cathedral structures, enjoy great music, and even participate in whatever humanitarian initiatives they may have. However, my personal cultural evolution tends to steer me toward the more non-theistic features of Unitarian-Universalism and the Ethical Society. Furthermore, the most revered or haloed aspects of religion in general can be found entirely outside of conventional churches, that is, the great humanitarian institutions dedicated to the betterment of society. Some of them are discussed in the following section.

Do Something Worthwhile

Everyone should be proud of their life-work accomplished, whether noteworthy or insignificant, and therefore feel that it is worthwhile. The satisfaction of an artist, plumber, writer, or any professional for that matter, whose work is the product of innate creative ability, should be the ultimate worthwhile objective. But when you realize that conditions, laws, attitudes, and other restraints may limit one's ultimate happiness and success in a life's work, then it becomes important to consider other productive activities as deserving of being called worthwhile, and they can as well be more enjoyable than "work." In this category I consider my long-time involvement with these organizations with which I have volunteered or to whom I have contributed. I can no more answer which of them is the most important than I could the same question about a three-legged stool.

Planned Parenthood

We are constantly reminded of the coming doom of society through global warming as a danger for the foreseeable future. Yet not even on the radar of most people are the Malthusian facts of overpopulation of the Earth and ultimately, the starvation and and/or extinction of the human race. Yet this could happen even sooner than the consequences of global warming, if not recognized.

Despite the potential for catastrophe, half the world's people are denied choices about their reproductive freedom. To attack this problem it is essential that birth control—the biological, scientific means and the moral imperative—be widely accepted, so that it becomes not only legal, but also morally proper, for women to plan or space their offspring in a healthful and economically sound manner. Lack of family planning options is tragically true for our poorest citizens, but most apparent among third-world countries, where population pressures are greatest. But fundamentalists, Catholics, and other hyper-devout groups work constantly to limit women's reproductive choices—leading us back to square one, the intersection of politics and democracy.

I first heard of Planned Parenthood in college after meeting Ruth. Her mother was a member, supporter, and volunteer in the organization. From its current descriptive publications one can learn that it was started by Margaret Sanger, the great crusader for human rights, about one hundred years ago, and "for more than 90 years has been the nation's leading sexual and reproductive health care provider and advocate…assisting millions of women and men in the U.S. and worldwide. With a presence in all 50 states and Washington, DC, Planned Parenthood has 95 affiliates, which operate more than 850 health centers."

Hillary Clinton, in her remarks to the 2009 Planned Parenthood Annual Meeting, said, "The reproductive rights movement was arguably one of the most transformational of the twentieth century. It changed the lives of millions of women and their families.... Yet we know that Margaret Sanger's work is still not done, here in the United States or around the world. There are still far too many women in too many places denied the right to plan and space their families and control their reproductive lives."

To simply agree with the noble objectives of this organization, as well as all others in the following descriptions, is clearly a way to help all humanity, but should be only the first step. Those who cannot physically volunteer can, at the very least, join and pay the relatively small annual membership fee in support of their help for others throughout the country and world. To do this, and to give more as finances allow (through charitable gift annuities, bequests, tax-free gifts, etc.), should go far to satisfy anyone's altruism (and even religiosity). No one should ever say, with such great organizations already established and ready to promote your hopes: "How can I do anything? What little does my two-cents-worth help? Why should I do anything?"

That last question is particularly pertinent today. At the time of writing, the U.S. Congress and state legislatures around the country, newly dominated by far-right Republicans and "tea-party" activists, have introduced and passed legislation barring Planned Parenthood from receiving public funds for any of the health services the organization provides. Given that only a tiny proportion (three percent) of Planned Parenthood's resources are used to provide (legal) abortions, while the vast majority of its spending goes to helping women avoid unwanted pregnncies, it is almost inevitable that such "Bills of Attainder" will result in more women becoming pregnant and, ultimately, leading to more abortions than at present.

Habitat for Humanity

This has been one of the most remarkable and successful philanthropic ventures of the last century. It began less than fifty years ago and in its first decade came to have international significance by creating affordable, well-built homes for people with limited resources. So far it has built or rehabilitated more than 400,000 homes housing more than 2.0 million people in more than 3,000 communities worldwide.

The organization was started by Millard and Linda Fuller in collaboration with Clarence Jordan near Americus, Georgia, just a few miles from the home of Jimmy Carter, who later became President of the United States and, equally important, a notable cooperator with and promoter of the venture. These pioneers were imbued with religious motivation, which must have contributed to their success, but the vast expansion across ethnic, religious, and political boundaries surely attests to the basic principles of cooperation and altruistic motivations originating long before modern religious organizations.

If one has a few hours, or perhaps a day off, it is very easy to find a local participating organization (typically a church) where one can volunteer to help on-site with construction, or through one of many of the subsidiary elements of building a home for a disadvantaged family. Even with no manual skills one can be of great use doing things that require very little instruction. Needless to say, financial contributions for the materials, no matter how small, are greatly enhanced by the free labor involved—usually the major expense of construction.

The Carter Center

Ever since Jimmy Carter was president I have been interested in the types of projects in which he was interested, amazed by their success, and finally satisfied by the fact that I may have been beneficial to some of the goals of his work. Not being able to actually participate by volunteer work, I started with small contributions, and as my gifts became more substantial, I was, not surprisingly, invited to the Carter Center for briefings on their work plus trips to Plains, Georgia, and tours of his home place.

It is difficult to capsulate the Center's profound activities throughout the world—eradicating horrible diseases such as Guinea worm in countries of West Africa and other endemic diseases in many other countries; mediating or resolving political conflicts; supervising elections and providing other advice to newly democratic countries—usually at their own invitation. It should be said that Jimmy Carter has been among the most capable and dedicated of all our past presidents in helping the disadvantaged people of our country and the world—particularly after leaving office.

American Friends Service Committee

As mentioned earlier, my father informed me of this organization which was formed during World War I to help conscientious objectors find ways to serve their country without taking lives in combat. In later years their work continued with a broadened statement of purpose: "…an organization that includes various faiths who are committed to social justice, peace and humanitarian service…. In collaboration with local communities and neighborhoods, AFSC's programs foster understanding and reconciliation, promote economic development and food security, educate the public on issues such as nuclear disarmament and the realities of military service, and help people take charge of their own destinies." To help them amplify this work, contributions and offers to volunteer are possible in many locations throughout the US and many foreign countries.

These four, of course, are randomly chosen targets of my volunteer efforts and support; every reader and every citizen searching for ways and means to make a lasting impact with something worthwhile will have his or her own list of causes, organizations, and areas of interest. But the value of one's contributions and involvement cannot be measured by tonnage or dollar amounts; "worthwhile" work is done whether one gives Bill Gates's Microsoft billions, my more modest contributions, or even time and support in lieu of cash. Indeed, driving a Meals on Wheels delivery car once a week is at least as fulfilling to the volunteer, and as helpful to the agency and its clients, as writing an annual check.

Here are a few reputable, important organizations that, for me, fall into different categories of "worthwhile-ness":

Protection of liberty and freedom from oppression for disadvantaged people everywhere
- American Civil Liberties Union
- Amnesty International
- Common Cause
- Public Citizen
- Southern Poverty Law Center

Enhancement of knowledge—particularly for the disadvantaged
- American Cancer Institute
- Berea College

Addressing problems of cultural evolution
- The Center for Inquiry
- The Humanist Foundation

Environmental protection and understanding
- American Society For the Prevention of Cruelty to Animals
- National Parks Conservation Association

Making Plans—to Say Goodbye

How one approaches the end of life varies widely among humans, yet in reality, for those who have any concerns, it is mostly governed by the cultural influence of religion. Religious leaders and organized religions have, since their earliest beginnings, capitalized on unfounded fears of the unknown, especially death, regardless of belief or lack of belief in an "afterlife." Whether or not there is any reality to—or future scientific proof of—an afterlife, seems to make no difference to most people. Those of many faiths who feel they have lived a reasonably good, holy, "spiritual" life seem confident they will be in good shape and comfortable when they reach "heaven." Those who have not—those whose consciences are troubling them—either discount the possibility of "hell" with the knowledge that their fun of living made it worthwhile, or hope they'll have time for a "deathbed conversion" before it's too late. (Those who believe in reincarnation strive to live so that this will be their final life—one lived well enough that they need not return to try again.)

Archeological evidence is replete with evidence of how primitive people were concerned about their life after death. One can only surmise that the spear buried with the corpse was thought to be useful later in self-defense, and the food in jars essential to allay hunger, and the other trappings of earthly life equally necessary in the next one. Many people view these artifacts in museums and calmly go on believing they will move on to some actual, physical "heaven" after death. That belief, of course, is comforting to those who have been deluded all their lives by their church's insistence on the joy of living in heaven as a reward for constraining their earthly behavior in conformity with the church's doctrine.

My mother gave me a very memorable and plausible understanding of "afterlife," despite her theistic outlook on religion. The gist of her pronouncement was, "Your heaven or hell will be represented in the attitudes of all the people you knew or influenced in your lifetime. You will be loved, admired, and revered in memories of those you treated well, physically helped, or were effectively guided by your own actions and works. You will be forgotten, detested, or hated by those to whom you acted cruelly or unjustly." Further, she implied, the finiteness of your after-life will vary proportionately with the magnitude of your actions.

As my education progressed through agriculture, biology, geology, chemistry, and other scientific disciplines, the scope of reality has helped me rationally accommodate my attitude about "afterlife." Also, science offers a rational explanation of the belief held by certain religions that it is possible for living creatures to live on infinitely in their environment in a biologically natural manner: If their remains are not embalmed, preserved in bronze caskets, or otherwise protected from normal biological destruction, their actual molecules or, at least, atoms will eventually be free to be utilized in the nutrition of plants and other organisms for their lives. This explanation could, of course, rationalize the Hindu concept of reincarnation (when they eat the grass over their decomposed bodies). And for me, this principle suits just fine—since it fits scientific discoveries.

My own graduate training revolved around mineral nutrition of plants. This discipline had proved the essential nature of various major elements, then minor elements, then trace elements (all obtained from the soil) for plant growth. The mineral elements contained in the human body include those necessary for plant growth and are available through decomposition in nature. Of course, cremation can render these elements available and readily transportable, which is the way I plan to be made available to Nature. I am hereby making the wish that my ashes be distributed in the near vicinity of some tall redwood trees in California, so that my atoms will be useful to these beautiful and majestic giants—as well as, perhaps, to some minor creatures: micro-organisms will devour traces of me and fertilize the soil; grasses will absorb those elements as they grow; small birds and chipmunks will eat the grass growing over the ashes, and then carry my atoms high up in the redwoods where they will live. I might not be able to enjoy the view myself, but how could one have a more wonderful and worthwhile afterlife?

Conclusions

Sequoia sempervirens (California redwood) overshadows the author

It is always a satisfying experience to come to the "end of the day," as our politicians are fond of reminding us, and discovering that you have been successful in uncovering some explanation—a problem's solution—for some "curiosity" or enigma that has troubled you or generations before. However, before elaborating on my "discoveries," the wonderful experience of describing happy memories of family events should be acknowledged. To have the urge—or face the economic necessity—to build homes for them, help them see nature, the world, and places of historical significance, was the most majestic part of my life.

I have tried to explain how my life—as that of all other "unknowing" biological entities— began, and how it developed under the guidance of my parents, who were in turn influenced by several generations of their forebears. With education in science, reading of history, and substantial curiosity about "rational" explanations of life processes, I came to my current position of "show-and-tell."

Humans, like other animals, are born with genetic combinations of chromosomes from parents. At first, and for quite a few years, their mental ability is essentially nil, but genetically transmitted "instincts" are there to begin with: they include aggression, fear, hunger, sex, etc. Religion has attempted for centuries to explain, rationalize, and encode systems for harmonizing behavior with these instinctive forces. These behaviors—as with ants, bees and other "social" creatures—are probably manifestations of Darwinian evolution, but cultural evolution has been discovered as a decisive element in the progress and/or decline of civilizations.

How does this happen? Quite simply. The human brain has evolved for hundreds of millennia with two outstanding characteristics: the incredible ability to *store* huge quantities of information (memory), and *imagination*. This latter feature is the crux of humankind's problem.

Imagination is unquestionably useful, considering the imaginative origins of ideas from thousands of inventors and visionaries who have contributed to the advances of our time. Unfortunately, it is also easily distracted towards hopeful fantasizing, often about ideas originally implanted by parents, other "teachers," and many early experiences. Such ideas are profoundly strengthened by the devotion of their adherents, through "faith" or imaginary "spiritual" concepts, to belief in things that are utterly untrue.

Since the time of Copernicus, science has dutifully chipped away at these fallacies. Yet even today, with thousands of educational institutions providing rational explanations of the vast disciplines of biology and the physical world, there are fundamentalists who deny the scientific evidence because of their "spiritual" convictions.

Much of our—and the world's—life revolves around the element of spirituality. This can mean, for most people, a comfortable, secure belief—faith—that some "higher" being or entity will look out for them, validate their behavior, and determine their ultimate destiny. In pursuit of what they deem the benefits of following these precepts, even mildly devout, non-fundamentalist individuals ignore evidence they can't refute in favor of convictions they cannot substantiate. The unbelievable, but comforting, precepts are preferable to the discomfort of the simple truth that we won't live forever, be purified of our errors and relieved of our human imperfections, or sit at the right hand of an all-knowing, all-seeing God.

To show the fallacies inherent in such "faith," I have tried, in a comparative fashion, to trace realities of my own life in such a way as to show how cultural evolution is the underlying reason for this dilemma in the last century. I do not intend to demean the term "spirituality" since it means so much to so many people; I have had similar sensations on seeing the beautiful features of nature, sensing the companionship of a dog or horse, experiencing the joy of personal creativity, or witnessing the smile or touch of someone helped by my act of kindness. Nevertheless, however benignly the term nourishes numbers of devout "souls," many are oblivious to the fact that the concept of "spirituality" is the refuge of misinformed fundamentalists, misled cultists, and fanatic terrorists as well. Conjecturally, the belief in "spiritual guidance" is simply a naive manifestation of Darwinian impulses for the survival of humanity; practically, its abuse could lead to humanity's annihilation. Philosophically, it is simply unbelievable.

End

NOTES

CHAPTER 1

1 (p. 6) Pennsylvania Dutch are a people of various religious affiliations, most of them Lutheran or Reformed, but many Anabaptists, non-Christian, and non-religious as well. They live primarily in Southeastern and South Central Pennsylvania in the area stretching in an arc from Bethlehem and Allentown through Reading, Lebanon, and Lancaster to York and Chambersburg. They can also be found throughout the Shenandoah Valley (the modern Interstate 81 corridor) in the adjacent states of Maryland, Virginia, West Virginia, and North Carolina, and in the large Amish and Mennonite communities in Mifflin County, Pennsylvania, in Ohio north and south of Youngstown and in Indiana around Elkhart. Their cultural traditions date back to the German immigrations to America in the 17th and 18th Centuries. (Wikipedia)

[2] (p. 12) Nashville's moniker, "the Athens of the South," influenced the choice of the Parthenon as the centerpiece of the "historic" park developed for the state's 1897 Centennial Fair. A number of buildings at the Exposition were based on ancient originals, but the Parthenon was the only one that was an exact reproduction. It was also the only one that was preserved by the city. Originally built of plaster, wood, and brick for the Centennial, the Parthenon was rebuilt on the same foundations, in concrete, in a project that started in 1920; the exterior was completed in 1925 and the interior in 1931.

Today, the Parthenon functions as an art museum, standing as the centerpiece of Centennial Park just west of downtown Nashville. Alan LeQuire's 1990 re-creation of the Athena Parthenos statue is the focus of the Parthenon, just as it was in ancient Greece. The 42-foot-high statue is gilded with more than eight pounds of gold leaf; she is cuirassed and helmeted, carries a shield on her left arm and a small (6-foot) statue of Victory in her right palm, and an equally colossal serpent rears its head between her and her shield. The building's decorations are polychromed to match, as closely as possible, the presumed original. Plaster replicas of the Parthenon Marbles found in the Naos (the east room of the main hall) are direct casts of the original sculptures that adorned the pediments of the Athenian Parthenon, dating back to 438 BC. Many fragments of the originals are housed in the British Museum in London; others are at the Acropolis Museum in Athens. (Wikipedia)

[3] (p. 13) James Weldon Johnson was a diplomat with the U.S. Foreign Service (1906-1912), author of *The Autobiography of an Ex-Colored Man* (published anonymously in 1912), *The Book of American Negro Spirituals* (1925), *Black Manhattan* (1930), his exploration of the contribution of African-Americans to the culture of New York, and *Negro Americans, What Now?* (1934), a book advocating civil rights for African Americans. In 1922, he edited *The Book of American Negro Poetry*, which the Academy of American Poets calls "a major contribution to the history of African-American literature." One of the works for which he is best remembered today, *God's Trombones: Seven Negro Sermons in Verse*, was published in 1927.

As an activist he was treasurer and then president of the Colored Republican Club, editorial page editor of the influential African American weekly *The New York Age*, and the national organizer and then national secretary of the National Association for the Advancement of Colored People (NAACP).

[4] (p. 14) see Richard Dawkins, *Viruses of the Mind*

CHAPTER 2

[5] (p. 17) Born as the son of a teacher at Strasbourg, Oberlin studied theology in his hometown. In 1766 he became pastor of Waldersbach, a remote and barren region in Steintal (Ban-de-la-Roche), a valley in the Vosges on the borders of Alsace and Lorraine. He set himself to better the material, and spiritual, condition of the inhabitants. He began by constructing roads through the valley and erecting bridges, inciting the peasantry to the enterprise by his personal example. He introduced an improved system of agriculture. Substantial cottages were erected, and various industrial arts were introduced. He founded an itinerant library, originated infant schools, and established an ordinary school at each of the five villages in the parish. In the work of education he received great assistance from his housekeeper, Louisa Scheppler (1763-1837). He died in 1826, and was interred with great manifestations of honor and affection at the village of Urbach. (Wikipedia)

[6] (p. 18) George William Norris (1861–1944) was a U.S. politician from Nebraska and a leader of progressive and liberal causes in Congress. He served five terms in the United States House of Representatives as a Republican from 1903 until 1913 and five terms in the United States Senate from 1913 until 1943, four terms as a Republican and the final term as an Independent. (Wikipedia)

[7] (p.18) Arthur Ernest Morgan (1878–1975) was a civil engineer and educator who designed the Miami Conservancy District flood control system and oversaw construction. He served as the president of Antioch College between 1920 and 1936. He was also the first chairman of Tennessee Valley Authority from 1933 until 1938. He was deeply committed to community and greatly interested in community settlements. As president of the TVA, he directed the building of dams and provided power as well as advancing a wide variety of cooperative enterprises and cottage industries.

[8] (p. 18) John Harcourt Morgan (no relation to Arthur), was the thirteenth president of the University of Tennessee (1919-34) and second chairman of the board of the Tennessee Valley Authority (1938-41). He was born in Kerrwood, Ontario, Canada in 1868, and after receiving a BS degree from the University of Toronto's Agricultural College at Guelph in 1889, he taught entomology at Louisiana State University, where he also researched cattle tick and boll weevil control and was credited with saving the cattle industry from the harmful effects of the tick. In 1905 Morgan moved to the University of Tennessee in Knoxville as professor of entomology and zoology, then as dean, and finally (1919) as president; in that role he enhanced the university's influence among Tennessee's farmers, adopting the motto "The State is the University's Campus," expanded the campus, and

quadrupled the student population. FDR appointed him to the TVA board in 1933, and he became the agency's agricultural specialist and its propagandist to the state's farmers. He and board member David Lilienthal promoted "grass roots democracy" to educate farmers in scientific agriculture and assure them that the TVA promoted their interests and not those of the federal government. Morgan was board chairman for three years and remained a director until 1948.

[9] (p. 18) David E. Lilienthal was a lawyer and orator appointed as the third member of the TVA board by President Roosevelt. While Arthur Morgan wanted to engage existing private power companies to distribute TVA power, Lilienthal, who neither respected nor trusted the private utilities, preferred Federal control and locally controlled rural power co-operatives. Their disagreement led Morgan to ask FDR not to reappoint Lilienthal, and he was supported by conservatives in Congress. But they could not substantiate Morgan's accusations of corruption, and in 1938 the president asked Morgan to resign from the TVA; when he refused, Roosevelt fired him.

[10] (p. 19) According to Erich Fromm, Bellamy's novel *Looking Backward* is "one of the most remarkable books ever published in America." It was the third largest bestseller of its time, after *Uncle Tom's Cabin* and *Ben-Hur: A Tale of the Christ*. In the book, Julian West, an upper-class man from 1887, awakes in 2000 from a hypnotic trance to find himself in a socialist utopia. The book influenced a large number of intellectuals, and "Bellamy Clubs" sprang up all over the United States to discuss the book's ideas as well as spawning several utopian communities.

[11] (p. 20) Herbert Spencer (1820–1903), English philosopher, sociologist, and classical liberal political theorist, developed an all-embracing conception of evolution as the progressive development of the physical world, biological organisms, the human mind, and human culture and societies. As a polymath, he contributed to a wide range of subjects, including ethics, religion, anthropology, economics, political theory, philosophy, biology, sociology, and psychology. During his lifetime he achieved tremendous authority, mainly in English-speaking academia. In 1902 he was nominated for the Nobel Prize in Literature. Spencer is best known for coining the concept "survival of the fittest" in his book *Principles of Biology* (1864), which he wrote after reading Charles Darwin's text *On the Origin of Species*. This term strongly suggests natural selection, yet as Spencer extended evolution into realms of sociology and ethics, he also made use of Lamarckism. (Wikipedia)

[12] (p. 20) Wendell Lewis Willkie (1892–1944) was a liberal Republican and a corporate lawyer who opposed New Deal policies that he considered inefficient and anti-business. He won the GOP nomination for president in 1940 and was badly defeated, but Roosevelt appointed Willkie an informal ambassador-at-large. In that role he travelled the world sharing a vision of "One World" free of imperialism and colonialism. He planned to run again in 1944, but his Republican support collapsed and he dropped out of the 1944 race; within a year he died of a heart attack at age 52.

Chapter 3

[13] (p. 26) Settlement Schools are social reform institutions established in rural Appalachia in the early 20th Century with the purpose of educating mountain children and improving their isolated rural communities. Settlement schools have played an important role in preserving and promoting the cultural heritage of southern and central Appalachia. Scholar David Whisnant has argued that settlement schools created a version of "traditional" Appalachian culture that appealed to outsiders but had little basis in the values of Appalachian people themselves. The schools were inspired by the Settlement movement that started in London in the late 19th Century and were represented in the United States by urban Settlement Houses, including Hull House in Chicago and the Henry Street Settlement in New York (Wikipedia)

[14] (p. 26) The Woman's Christian Temperance Union is the oldest non-sectarian women's organization in the world. Organized in Cleveland, OH in 1874, the group entered saloons singing, praying, and urging saloon keepers to stop selling alcohol. It was inspired by the Greek writer Xenophon, who defined temperance as "moderation in all things healthful; total abstinence from all things harmful." The WCTU perceived alcoholism and other social ills as the consequence of larger social problems rather than as a personal weakness or failing; thus members also focused on social issues such as prostitution, public health, sanitation, labor rights, and, in later years, women's suffrage.

[15] (p. 26) As the 1928 Republican presidential candidate, former Commerce Secretary Herbert Hoover campaigned against Democrat Alfred E. Smith on a platform of prosperity led by efficient business practices. Both men supported business, family farmers, immigration reform, and isolationism in the aftermath of World War I. But Hoover claimed to support Prohibition, calling it a "noble experiment," though he was rumored to enjoy cocktails and wine throughout the 1920s with visits to the "foreign soil" of the Belgian Embassy. Hoover's strong business credentials and Prohibitionist stance allowed his supporters, including the WCTU, to attack Smith as a "wet" while avoiding direct attacks on his Catholicism, leading to Hoover's winning with 58 percent of the vote. Hoover promised that "We in America today are nearer to the final triumph over poverty than ever before in the history of any land," but less than a year after his election, the stock market crashed and the nation entered the Great Depression.

[16] (p. 27) In mathematics, the Pythagorean theorem is the relation among the three sides of a right triangle. It states that in any right triangle, the square of the hypotenuse (the side opposite the right angle) is equal to the sum of the squares of the other two sides (the sides that meet at a right angle). The theorem is often called the Pythagorean equation: $a^2 + b^2 = c^2$ where c is the length of the hypotenuse and a and b are the two short sides.

[17] (p. 28) Oberlin, whose founders bragged that "Oberlin is peculiar in that which is good," was the first college in the United States (in 1835) to regularly admit African American students and the first to admit women (1837). The college was listed as a National Historic

Landmark on December 21, 1965 for its significance in admitting African Americans and women. It also had a reputation as a hotbed of abolitionism, serving as a stop along the Underground Railroad.

Antioch, a private, independent liberal arts college in Yellow Springs, Ohio, opened in 1853 under the leadership of education reformer Horace Mann. From 1921 to 2008, students were required to include practical work experience with classroom learning, but by 2007 the college was virtually broke. In July 2008 the Board of Trustees suspended operations and transferred all assets—the campus, a $20 million endowment, and the *Antioch Review*—to a separate entity that reopened in September 2011. The incoming class of 35 students is approximately the same size as the original 1853 freshman class.

Beloit College was chartered in 1846 by a group of New Englanders who had moved to the Wisconsin Territory; it was informally associated with the New England Congregationalist tradition. The first building, which is still in use, was built in 1847; the first president was Yale alumnus Aaron Lucius Chapin (1849-1886). Its enrollment reached 1,000 students only with the influx of World War II veterans in 1945-1946. For several years (1964-1977), it followed the "Beloit Plan," a year-round curriculum balancing three terms of classroom work with a "field term" off campus.

Chapter 4

[18] (p. 34) Quakers are members of the Religious Society of Friends, a denomination that emerged in England in the mid-1600s and is practiced today around the world; central to the faith are pacifism, social equality, integrity, and simplicity.

[19] (p. 35) Derivation of the term "Winkeltablen charts" is uncertain—perhaps just a whimsical notion that they had been constructed by German mathematician/astronomers. In any case, they were extensive, multi-volume, extremely accurate tables of numbers to show exactly where you were in the world, if you had the altitude and azimuth and correct time of night for a given star, planet, or the sun (as obtained with a sextant or octant).

[20] (p. 36) Bernoulli's principle is named after the Dutch-Swiss mathematician Daniel Bernoulli, who published his principle in his book *Hydrodynamica* in 1738. In fluid dynamics, Bernoulli's principle states that for an inviscid flow, an increase in the speed of the fluid occurs simultaneously with a decrease in pressure or a decrease in the fluid's potential energy. In accord with the principle, in the case of an airfoil of most aircraft wings, the upper surface is curved while the lower surface is flat. As the wing moves rapidly forward the air has to move faster over the upper surface (since it has to go farther in a curve than in a straight line) than the lower, thus creating a lowered pressure (upward suction) on the upper surface relative to the more undisturbed lower surface, and the wings consequently lift the whole plane.

[21] (p. 36) The U.S. military service had ROTC (Reserve Officer Training Corps) established in most major universities and some colleges throughout the country. Traditionally, this

program supplied military classes, both academic and physical, that would qualify a person to be an officer, as opposed to direct enlistment as a non-commissioned private or midshipman in the service, i.e. the same rank that would be obtained at West Point or Annapolis.

[22] (p. 36) The Piper J-3 Cub, built between 1937 and 1947 by Piper Aircraft, has single tandem seating and was designed for flight training. The Piper J-3 Cub was used to train 80 percent of all American military pilots during World War II. Because of its widespread familiarity, affordability, light weight and maneuverability, the plane became the most popular and widely owned light aircraft of its time.

Chapter 5

[23] (p. 45) The safety, economy and effective utility of every consumer product should be, and has been to a large extent, insured by our government, as compared with many less developed countries. Unfortunately, these ideals have been frequently compromised politically by budget cuts in numbers of inspectors, training of inspectors, and all sorts of oversight of manufacturers' claims and production of products. Consequently, when an agricultural worker is sickened or killed by misuse of a pesticide; or consumers are made ill from misuse or insufficient washing or decontamination of products; or information on safer alternative products and practices are unavailable to the public, the agricultural chemical industry get the black eye, not the politicians.

[24] (p. 49) Both cults and sects have a long tradition within established religion, ranging from the cults of individual gods and goddesses in Greek and Roman pantheism to the numerous sects that defined early Judaism and centuries of Christian beliefs. The main branches of Judaism—orthodox, conservative, and reform—are considered sects by some, and many consider smaller groups, like the various Satmar, Lubavitch, and Gerrer Hasidim, to be sects or, in the case of the Lubavitcher, a cult of the new Messiah. Similarly the many Christian denominations that grew out of the Reformation were deemed sects by the Catholic authorities, though they are now mainstream enough that their members view smaller groups, such as snake-handlers and evangelicals and charismatics, as sects. One definition of a cult is a group founded by a charismatic leader who wields absolute authority over dogma, practice, and, usually, his followers' behavior; when he (or rarely she) dies, the cult often founders as well. If it survives long enough to take root, grow new leadership, and attract new followers after the founder's death or departure, it might, if accepted by its mainstream cousins, become a sect or even a denomination of its own. Christianity, after all, began as nothing more than a cult of Jesus, then became a sect of Judaism, and finally emerged as a separate religious identity.

[25] (p. 49) Two long-established religious traditions, Unitarian and Universalist, merged in 1961 after decades of declining membership in each one. Their compatibility was found in their disagreement with most protestant faiths, in that Unitarians denied the Trinitarian creed including the divinity of Jesus, and Universalists maintained that salvation was

available to all, without the need for Jesus as an intercessor with God. As followers of a creedless religion, many Unitarian-Universalists are atheists or agnostics; nearly all UU theists adhere to strict monotheism, maintaining that Jesus was a great man and a prophet of God, perhaps even a supernatural being, but not God himself. They believe Jesus did not claim to be God, and that his teachings did not suggest the existence of a triune God. Many, even most, UUs believe in the moral authority, but almost none in the divinity, of Jesus.

[26] (p. 50) Transcendentalism is a term associated with a group of new ideas in literature and philosophy that emerged in New England in the early-to-middle 19th century. It is sometimes called American Transcendentalism to distinguish it from other uses of the word transcendental. The movement developed in the 1830s and '40s as a protest against the general state of culture and society, and in particular, the state of intellectualism at Harvard College and the doctrine of the Unitarian church taught at Harvard Divinity School. Among transcendentalists' core beliefs was the belief in an ideal spiritual state that "transcends" the physical and empirical and is realized only through the individual's intuition, rather than through the doctrines of established religions.

CHAPTER 6

[27] (p. 54) Ethical Culture, or the Ethical Culture Movement, is an ethical, educational, and religious movement that was established by Felix Adler in 1876. Individual chapter organizations are generically referred to as Ethical Societies, though their names may include "Ethical Society," "Ethical Culture Society," "Society for Ethical Culture," "Ethical Humanist Society," or other variations on the theme of "Ethical." Ethical Culture is premised on the idea that honoring and living in accordance with ethical principles is central to what it takes to live meaningful and fulfilling lives, and to creating a world that is good for all. Practitioners of Ethical Culture focus on supporting one another in becoming better people, and on doing good in the world.

[28] (p. 56) Corticosteroids are a class of steroid hormones that are produced in the adrenal cortex. Corticosteroids are involved in a wide range of physiologic systems such as stress response, immune response and regulation of inflammation, carbohydrate metabolism, protein catabolism, blood electrolyte levels, and behavior.

[29] (p. 56) Charles Warren Thornthwaite (March 7, 1899 - June 11, 1963) was an American geographer and climatologist. He is best known for devising a climate classification system, published in 1948, that is still in use around the world, and also for his detailed water budget computations of potential evapotranspiration. He was Professor of Climatology at Johns Hopkins University, adjunct professor at Drexel University, President of the Commission for Climatology of the World Meteorological Organization, a recipient of the Outstanding Achievement Award of the Association of American Geographers, and the Cullum Medal from the American Geographical Society.

[30] (p. 57) Leaf development: index of plant response to environmental factors. 1964. J. J. Higgins, J. R. Haun, and E. James Koch. Agronomy Journal Vol. 56:489-492.

[31] (p. 57) *Crambe abysinica* is an oilseed crop native to the Mediterranean area. According to the *Alternative Field Crops Manual*, it is used as an industrial lubricant, a corrosion inhibitor, and as an ingredient in the manufacture of synthetic rubber. It can also be used in surfactants and slip and coating agents.

[32] (p. 57) Kenaf (*Hibiscus cannabinus L*) is considered one of the most promising alternatives to virgin soft- and hardwoods for paper production. A herbaceous annual related to cotton and okra, kenaf is a member of the mallow family indigenous to West Africa. The US Department of Agriculture (USDA) began researching kenaf in the 1940s, when World War II put a stop to jute imports from Asia. In 1960, the USDA chose kenaf from among five hundred candidates as the most promising non-wood fiber for pulp and paper production. After much research and numerous trials runs, kenaf paper is now available from several commercial retailers and is being used by major corporations, printing and graphics firms and publishers. http://www.visionpaper.com/kenaf2.html

[33] (p. 57) *Tephrosia vogelii* is a small tree or shrub with insecticidal properties in its foliage, used in its native Africa and in Indonesia, the Philippines, and Malaysia. Its leaves contain compounds used as insecticides against lice, felas, and ticks, as well as for treatment of skin and digestive diseases. The plant is a good nitrogen-fixing species helpful in providing "green manure" to improve the soil.

Chapter 7

[34] (p. 66) The Haun Growth Scale (Haun, 1973) is far more precise than other commonly used scales. The Haun scale assigns consecutive numbers to main stem leaves in the order in which they appear. When the first leaf is fully developed, the plant is at stage 1, and so on through stage 8. Each leaf is fully developed when the next leaf is visible in the rolled part of the leaf. For example, leaf 2 is fully developed when the third leaf is visible in the rolled part of leaf 1. www.ndawn.ndsu.nodak.edu/help.html?topic=wheatgold-info

Chapter 11

[35] (p. 139) The Mondragón cooperatives were established in 1956 by a Catholic priest in the Basque region of Spain, Father Don José Arizmendi, as a way to overcome the unemployment and poverty of the region. He began by holding workshops and educational "study circles," through which emerged a philosophical approach of putting workers rights and welfare above all other considerations. Growth was a secondary consideration, aimed not at improving profits and returns but rather increasing employment and improving job security. Today Mondragón cooperatives comprise more than 100 cooperative enterprises as well as another hundred subsidiary businesses that Mondragón has bought with the aim of converting them to the cooperative model.

[36] (p. 140) An excellent portrait and analysis of the Bank of North Dakota can be found in "Socialism Thrives in North Dakota," *Newsweek*, May 3, 2010.

[37] (p. 146) See bibliography for numerous books on these subjects by Herrick, Kurtz,

Moran, and the Council for Secular Humanism.

[38] (p. 146) The book is an anthology of articles & interviews that have appeared in *Free Inquiry* magazine, published by The Humanist Society, Matt Cherry, Tom Flynn, & Timothy Madigan, editors.

[39] (p. 149) Einstein's Theory of Relativity states, among other postulates, that energy (E) equals mass (m) multiplied by the square of the speed of light (c^2); it is inextricably linked with the related postulate that nothing in the universe has or can have a greater velocity than light (in a vacuum), which is, in layman's terms, pure energy made visible. But as this book went to press, the European Center for Nuclear Research (CERN) in Geneva, Switzerland announced that it had measured the speed of neutrinos in its accelerator at 60 nanoseconds faster than the speed of light. Headlines announced that "Einstein's theory falls"; but CERN's assertion will be examined, challenged, and reproduced in CERN's and other accelerators before it can be confirmed or is refuted. If it is confirmed, scientists will eagerly rethink many other propositions and theories that flow from $E=mc^2$, and our understanding of the workings of the universe will be not shattered by a "loss of faith," but enhanced by growth of knowledge.

BIBLIOGRAPHY

In addition to the publications cited in the text, this list contains other suggested reading to enlarge on stated views and concepts of various authors, particularly of Richard Dawkins, Daniel Dennett, Jimmy Carter, Paul Kurtz, and E.O. Wilson. These are included to acknowledge—with gratitude—the development of my personal concepts, seemingly related but chronologically independent.

Anderson, Walter Truett. 1995. *The Truth about The Truth.* Edited by Walter Truett Anderson. Jeremy F. Tarcher/Putnam, a member of Penguin Putnam Inc, New York, NY. 260 pp.

Balmer, Randall. 2006. *Thy Kingdom Come: How the Religious Right Distorts the Faith and Threatens America.* Basic Books, New York, NY. 242 pp.

Barker, Dan. 2008. *Godless: How an Evangelical Preacher Became One of America's Leading Atheists.* Ulysses Press. Berkeley, CA. 374 pp.

Barton, Bruce, with introduction by Richard M. Fried. 2000. *The Man Nobody Knows.* (first published by the Bobbs-Merrill Co. in 1925. Indianapolis), Ivan R. Dee, Chicago, IL. 102 pp.

Becker, Ernest. 1971. *The Birth and Death of Meaning: An interdisciplinary perspective on the problem of man.* Second edition. The Free Press, New York, NY. 228 pp.

Bellamy, Edward. 1888. *Looking Backward: 2000-1887.* Ticknor and Company, Boston. 1996. Unabridged republication, Dover Publications, Inc., New York, NY. 165pp.

Berry, Wendell. 2001. *In the Presence of Fear.* The Orion Society, Great Barrington, MA. 44 pp.

Buglisi, Vincent. 2001. *The Betrayal of America: How the Supreme Court Undermined the Constitution and Chose our President.* Thunder's Mouth Press/Nation Books, New York, NY. 166 pp.

Carter, Jimmy. 1993. *The Blood of Abraham: Insights Into the Middle East.* The University of Arkansas Press, Fayetteville, AR. 243 pp.

_____. 2005. *Our Endangered Values: America's Moral Crisis.* Simon & Schuster, New York, NY. 212 pp.

_____. 2006. *Palestine: Peace Not Apartheid.* Simon & Schuster, New York, NY. 264 pp.

_____. 2007. *Beyond the White House: Waging Peace, Fighting Disease, Building Hope.* Simon & Schuster, New York, NY. 272 pp.

Cassirer, Ernst (Translated by Susanne K. Langer). 1946. *Language And Myth.* Dover Publications Inc., New York, NY. 103 pp.

_____. 1965. *An Essay on Man—An Introduction to a Philosophy of Human Culture.* Yale University Press, New Haven, CT. 237 pp.

Clark, Thomas W. 2007. *Encountering Naturalism: A Worldview and Its Uses.* Center for Naturalism. Somerville, MA. 101 pp.

Coyne, J.A. 2009. *Why Evolution Is True.* Viking/Penguin Group, New York, NY. 309 pp.

Council for Secular Humanism. 1997. *Imagine There's No Heaven: Voices of Secular Humanism.* Edited by Matt Cherry, Tom Flynn, and Timothy Madigan. Council for Secular Humanism, Amherst, NY. 103 pp.

Creekmore, Marion Jr. 2006. *A Moment of Crisis: Jimmy Carter, the Power of a Peacemaker, and North Korea's Nuclear Ambitions.* BBS Public Affairs, New York, NY. 406 pp.

Cunningham, George C. 2010. *Decoding the Language of God: Can a Scientist Really Be a Believer? A Geneticist Responds to Francis Collins.* Prometheus Books, Amherst, NY. 269 pp.

Davis, Kenneth S. 2000. *FDR: The War President, 1940-1943.* Random House, Inc., New York, NY. 848 pp.

Dawkins, Richard. 1989. *The Selfish Gene.* Oxford University Press USA, New York, NY. 360 pp.

_____, 2004. *The Ancestor's Tale.* Houghton Mifflin Company, New York, NY. 673 pp.

_____, 2006. *The God Delusion.* Houghton Mifflin Company, New York, NY. 463 pp.

_____, 2009. *The Greatest Show On Earth: The Evidence For Evolution.* Free Press, New York, NY. 470 pp.

Dees, Morris. 2001. *A Lawyer's Journey: The Morris Dees Story.* American Bar Association, Chicago, IL. 365 pp.

Dennett, Daniel C. 1991. *Consciousness Explained.* Little, Brown and Company, Boston, MA. 511 pp.

_____, 1995. *Darwin's Dangerous Idea, Evolution and the Meaning of Life.* Simon & Schuster Paperbacks, New York, NY. 586 pp.

_____, 2006. *Breaking The Spell: Religion as a Natural Phenomenon.* Viking, New York, NY. 448 pp.

Dewey, John. 1989. *Freedom and Culture.* Prometheus Books, Amherst, NY. 134 pp.

Dobzhansky, Theodosius. 1967. *The Biology of Ultimate Concern.* The New American Library, New York, NY. 152 pp.

Durant, Will. 2001. *Heroes of History: A Brief History of Civilization from Ancient Times to the Dawn of the Modern Age.* Simon & Schuster, New York, NY. 348 pp.

_____. 2002. *The Greatest Minds and Ideas of All Time.* Compiled and edited by John Little. Simon & Schuster, New York, NY. 127 pp.

Dutton, William S. 1951. *DuPont: One Hundred and Fifty Years.* Charles Scribner's Sons, New York, NY. 408 pp.

Emerson, Ralph Waldo, edited and with an introduction by Richard Whelan. 1991. *Self Reliance.* Bell Tower, New York, NY. 207 pp.

Fairchild, David. 1938. *The Word Was My Garden: Travels of a Plant Explorer.* Scribner's & Sons, New York, NY.

Flynn, Tom. 2004. *Nothing Sacred.* Prometheus Books, Amherst, NY. 474 pp.

Frost, S. E., Jr. 1942, 1962. *Basic Teachings Of The Great Philosophers.* Anchor Books-

Doubleday, New York, NY. 301 pp.

Gaylor, Annie Laurie, ed. 1997. *Women Without Superstition: No Gods, No Masters: The Collected Writings of Women Freethinkers of the Nineteenth & Twentieth Centuries.* Freedom From Religion Foundation, Madison, WI. 680 pp.

Goldstein, Rebecca Newberger. 2006. *Betraying Spinoza: The Renegade Jew Who Gave Us Modernity.* Nextbook-Schocken, New York, NY. 287 pp.

Goodwin, Doris Kearns. 1995. *No Ordinary Time: Franklin and Eleanor Roosevelt: The Home Front in World War II.* A Touchstone Book, Published by Simon & Schuster, New York, NY. 759 pp.

Harris, Sam. 2005. *The End Of Faith: Religion, Terror, and the Future of Reason.* W. W. Norton & Company, New York, NY. 348.

Haught, James A. 1996. *2000 Years of Disbelief: Famous People with the Courage to Doubt.* Prometheus Books, Amherst, NY. 334 pp.

Henderson, John A. and Craig Gurgew. 2007. *Judging God.* Parkway Publishers, Inc., Boone, NC. 294 pp.

Higgins, Joseph J, Joseph R. Haun, and E. J. Koch. 1964. Leaf Development: Index of Plant Response to Environmental Factors, *Agronomy Journal*, Vol. 56:489-492, 1964.

Hitchens, Christopher. 2007. *God is NOT Great: How Religion Poisons Everything.* Hachette Books Group USA, New York, NY. 307 pp.

———, 2007. *The Portable Atheist: Essential Readings for the Nonbeliever.* Da Capo Press, Philadelphia, PA. 499 pp.

Hutchins, Jeffrey Melvin. 2005. *A Press Conference with God: An Atheist Talks to God and Gets Answers to Your Questions.* Infinity, West Conshohocken, PA 268 pp.

Jackson, Robert H. 2003. *That Man: An Insider's Portrait of Franklin D. Roosevelt.* Oxford University Press USA, New York, NY. 290 pp.

Ingersoll, Robert G. 1990. *On the Gods and Other Essays.* Prometheus Books, Buffalo, NY. 177 pp.

———. 2004. *Superstition and Other Essays.* Prometheus Books. Buffalo, NY. 169 pp.

———. 2005. *What's God Got to Do With It? Robert Ingersoll on Free Thought, Honest Talk, and the Separation of Church and State.* Edited & with an introduction by Tim Page. Steerforth Press, Hanover, NH. 137 pp.

Karabell, Zachary. 2000. *The Last Campaign: How Harry Truman Won the 1948 Election.* Alfred A. Knopf, New York, NY. 308 pp.

Kowalski, Gary. 1991. *The Souls of Animals.* Stillpoint Publishing, Walpole, NH. 114 pp.

Kreig, Margaret B. 1964. *Green Medicine: The Search for Plants that Heal.* Rand McNally & Company, New York, NY. 462 pp.

Kurtz, Paul. 1991. *The Transcendental Temptation: A Critique of Religion and the Paranormal.* Prometheus Books, Amherst, NY. 500 pp.

———. 1994. *Living Without Religion: Eupraxophy.* Prometheus Books, Amherst, New York, NY. 159pp.

———. 1997. *The Courage to Become: The Virtues of Humanism.* Praeger, Westport,

CT. 138 pp.

———. 2003. *Science and Religion: Are They Compatible?* Prometheus Books, Amherst, NY. 366 pp.

———. 2004. *Affirmations: Joyful and Creative Exuberance.* Prometheus Books, Amherst, NY. 119 pp.

———. 2006, 2007. *What is Secular Humanism?* Prometheus Books, Amherst, New York, NY. 42 and 62 pp.

Larson, Orvin. 1993. *American Infidel: Robert G. Ingersoll.* Freedom from Religion Foundation, Madison, WI. 315 pp.

Lilienthal, David E. 1944. *TVA: Democracy on the March.* Pocket Books, Inc., New York, NY. 248 pp.

———. 1984. *The Journals of David E. Lilienthal, Vol. I: The TVA Years, 1939-45.* Harper & Row, New York, Evanston, and London. 734 pp.

Lorenz, Konrad (translated by Marjorie Kerr Wilson). 1963. *On Aggression.* Harcourt Brace & Company. New York, NY. 306 pp.

Lynn, Barry W. 2006. *Piety & Politics: The Right-Wing Assault on Religious Freedom.* Harmony Books, New York, NY. 261 pp.

Martin, Michael & Ricki Monnier, eds. 2003. *The Impossibility of God.* Prometheus Books, Amherst, NY. 438 pp.

McCumber, John. 2000. *Philosophy and Freedom.* Indiana University Press, Bloomington, IN & Indianapolis, IN. 191 pp.

Morgan, Arthur E. 1944. *Edward Bellamy.* Columbia University Press, New York, NY. 468 pp.

———. 1968. *Observations.* The Antioch Press, Yellow Springs, OH. 324 pp.

———. 1971. *Dams and Other Disasters: A Century of the Army Corps of Engineers in Civil Works.* Porter Sargent Publishers, Boston, MA. 422 pp.

Obama, Barack. 2006. *The Audicity of Hope: Thoughts on Reclaiming the American Dream.* Crown Publishers, New York, NY. 375 pp.

Paine, Thomas. 1794-95. *The Age of Reason.* Published by the author in two parts, 1794 and 1795; published by G. P. Putnam's Sons, New York, NY, 1890. 237 pp.

Phillips, Kevin. 2006. *American Theocracy: The Peril and Politics of Radical Religion, Oil, and Borrowed Money in the 21st Century.* Penguin Group, New York, NY. 462 pp.

Pigliucci, Massimo. 2002. *Denying Evolution: Creationism, Scientism, and the Nature of Science.* Sinauer Associates, Sunderland, MA. 337 pp.

Pinker, Steven. 1997. *How the Mind Works.* W. W. Norton & Company, New York, NY. 660 pp.

———. 2002. *The Blank Slate: The Modern Denial of Human Nature.* Viking Press, New York, NY. 509 pp.

Roosevelt. Franklin D. 1934. *On Our Way.* The John Day Company, New York, NY. 300 pp.

Sagan, Carl, and Ann Druyan. 1993. *Shadows of Forgotten Ancestors.* Ballantine Books, New York, NY. 528 pp.

_____. 1996. *The Demon-Haunted World: Science as a Candle in the Dark.* Ballantine Books, New York, NY. 480 pp.

Sanger, Margaret. 1915. "Family Limitation," self-published, New York, NY.

Schram, Martin. 1995. *Speaking Freely: Former Members of Congress Talk About Money in Politics.* Center for Responsive Politics. Washington, DC. 157 pp.

Sharlet, Jeff. 2009. *The Family: The Secret Fundamentalism at the Heart of American Power.* HarperCollins Publishers, New York, NY. 454 pp.

_____. 2010. *C Street: The Fundamentalist Threat to American Democracy.* Little, Brown and Company, New York, NY. 344 pp.

Smith, Maureen. 1997. *The U.S. Paper Industry and Sustainable Production.* Massachusetts Institute of Technology Press, Boston, MA. 303 pp.

Sweeney, Julia. 2006. *Letting Go of God.* Audio Cd, Indefatigable, Inc. London. Two-disc set.

Tarnas, Richard. 1991. *The Passion of the Western Mind: Understanding the Ideas That Have Shaped Our World View.* Ballantine Books, New York, NY. 544 pp.

Tobin, James. 2001. *Great Projects: The Epic Story of the Building of America, from the Taming of the Mississippi to the Invention of the Internet.* The Free Press of Simon & Schuster, Inc., New York, NY. 322 pp.

Wade, Nicholas. 2006. *Before the Dawn: Recovering the Lost History of our Ancestors.* Penguin Books, New York, NY. 314 pp.

Whitman, Walt. Originally published 1855, this edition 2009. *Leaves of Grass.* American Renaissance Books, Nashville, TN. 128 pp.

Wilson, E. O. 1975. *Sociobiology: The New Synthesis.* Belknap Press of Harvard University Press, Cambridge, MA. 697 pp.

_____. 1978, 2004. *On Human Nature.* Harvard University Press, Cambridge, MA. 260 pp.

_____. 1992, 1999. *The Diversity of Life.* W. W. Norton & Company, New York, NY. 424 pp.

_____. 1995. *Naturalist.* Warner Books, New York, NY. 380 pp.

_____. 1998. *Consilience.* Alfred A. Knopf, New York, NY. 332 pp.

Appendix A
Partial list of J. R. Haun's published works

A preliminary study of the mineral nutrition of hydrangeas. 1950. J. B. Shanks, J. R. Haun, and C. B. Link. *Proceedings*, American Society Horticultural Science (This paper was given recognition by the awards committee of the ASHS.) 56: pp 457-465.

Rooting response of geranium cuttings as influenced by nitrogen, phosphorus, and potassium nutrition of the stock plant. 1951. J. R. Haun and P. W. Cornell. *Proceedings*, American Society Horticultural Science 58: pp 317-323.

Copper nutrition of plants. 1951. J. R. Haun. PhD thesis University of Maryland.

Translocation of 3-(p-chlorophenyl)-1, 1-Dimethylurea in plants. 1954. J. R. Haun and J. H. Peterson. *Weeds*. (This paper was an invitational presentation at the first National Weed Control Conference.) 3: pp 177-187.

Cacao seedlings production and distribution through plant quarantine. 1960. H. H. Fisher and J. R. Haun. *Cacao* 5:4 pp 1-9.

Mineral-deficiency symptoms in *Dioscorea composita*. 1961. J. G. Gosselink, M. H. Gaskins, and J. R. Haun. *Proceedings* of Caribbean Region, American Society for Horticultural Science IX Annual Meeting, Miami, March 19-25. Vol 5. pp 59-63.

Bamboo in the United States; description, culture and utilization (with key to the genera by F. A. McClure). 1961. R. A. Young and J. R. Haun. *USDA Agriculture Handbook No. 193.*

Crambe: A potential new crop for industrial and feed uses. 1962. Anonymous. *USDA-ARS 34-42.*

Factors involved in the vegetative propagation of *Dioscorea spiculiflora* Hemsl. from vines. 1962. W. H. Preston, Jr. and J. R. Haun. *Proceedings*, American Society for Horticultural Science Vol. 80. pp 417-429.

Relationships of temperature and photoperiod to growth, flowering, senescence, and dormancy of *Dioscorea spiculiflora*. 1963. W. H. Preston, Jr. and J. R. Haun. *Botany Gazette*, Vol. 124, No.5. pp 346-353.

Quantitative morphology: a method for improving crop production. 1964. J. R. Haun. *Journal of the American Society of Farm Managers and Rural Appraisers*. Vol. XXVII No. 1. pp 42-44.

Leaf development: index of plant response to environmental factors. 1964. J. J. Higgins, J. R. Haun, and E. James Koch. *Agronomy Journal* Vol. 56:489-492.

Crop production analysis: the measurement and evaluation of plant response to environment. 1964. J. R. Haun. *Proceedings*, thirteenth annual meeting of the Agriculture Research Institute of the National Acadedmy of Science, National Research Council. Oct 12-13, 1964. Washington, D. C.

Culture of Temperate Zone Bamboo. 1964. W. O. Hawley, H. I. DeRigo and J. R. Haun. *American Nurseryman* Vol. 69, No.2.

Potential Pulp Crops. 1964. G. A. White and J. R. Haun. *Crops and Soils*, Vol. 16, No.8.

Several aspects of growth, development and Sapogenin yield of tubers of *Dioscorea spiculiflora*. 1964. W. H. Preston, Jr., J. R. Haun, J. W. Garvin, and R. J. Daum. *Economics of Botany* Vol. 18, No.4., pp 323-328.

Oil seed composition of two species of *Dimorphotheca* grown at five locations in the United States. 1965. R. E. Knowles, L. A. Goldblatt, G. O. Kohler, S. J. Toy, and J. R. Haun. *Economics of Botany* Vol. 19, No.3, pp 262-266.

Growing *Crotalaria juncea*, a multi-purpose legume, for paper pulp. 1965. George A. White and J. R. Haun. *Economics of Botany* Vol. 19, No.2., pp 175-183.

Fiber and papermaking characteristics of Bamboo. 1966. J. R. Haun, T. F. Clark, and George A. White. *USDA-ARS Bulletin No. 1361*.

Detection and evaluation of plant growth responses to environmental conditions. 1971. A. J. Lewis III and J. R. Haun. *American Journal of Botany* 58: 394-400.

Interaction of soil temperature and day length on the growth and flowering of carnations. 1972. C. R. Johnson and J. R. Haun. *Horticultural Science* 7: 114-116.

Analysis of crop-environment relationships and elaboration of the temperature response in snap bean production. 1972. J. R. Haun, A. J. Lewis III, S. J. Tsao, R. A. Baumgardner, and D. O. Ezell. *Technical Bulletin 1040* S. C. Agricultural Experimental Station 35 pp.

Visual quantification of wheat development. 1973. J. R. Haun. *Agronomy Journal*. 65: 116-119.

Climatic plant-harvest schedule for snap beans in coastal plains of South Carolina. *Circular 167*. S. C. Agricultural Experimental Station 18 pp. 1973.

Determination of wheat growth-environment relationships. 1973. J. R. Haun. *Agronomy Journal* 65:813 - 816.

Prediction of spring wheat yields from temperature and precipitation data. 1973. J. R. Haun. *Agronomy Journal* 66:405-409.

Evaluation of wheat development relative to environment from quantitative morphological data. 1973. *Proceedings* of Symposium on Agrometeorology of the Wheat Crop sponsored by the World Meteorological Organization in cooperation with The Federal Republic of Germany. Presented October 22-27, 1973).

Potato growth-environment relationships. 1976. J. R. Haun. *Agricultural Meteorology* 15:325-332.

Chemical pinching of "Hetzi II" Holly with EHPP. 1975. A. J. Lewis, III, and J. R. Haun. *Horticultural Science* 10: 180.

Development of models for specific crop calendar events. 1975. J. R. Haun. *International Journal of Biometeorology*. 20:3-10.

If you know the weather, you can predict the yield. 1978. J. R. Haun. *Crops & Soils*. 31:7.

Early prediction of corn yields from daily weather data and single predetermined seasonal constants. 1982. J. R. Haun. *Agricultural Meteorology* 27:191-207.

Relationship of daily growth and development of peach leaves and fruit to environmental factors. 1983. J.R. Haun and D.C. Coston, Jr. *American Society of Horticultural*

Science. 108:666-671.

Mathematical models in agrometeorology. 1983. J. R. Haun. *CAgM Report* No. 14, World Meteorological Organization, Geneva, Switzerland.

Quantification of maize growth: environment relationships. 1984. *Wissenschaftliche Zeitschrift* der Humboldt-Universitat zu Berlin, Math. -Nat. R. XXXIII (1984) 4:369-370.

APPENDIX B

2. Our wealth of knowledge of the world continues to expand.
   It is based upon the facts of science we can understand.
   Carbon dated fossils show what lived all over our great land.
   Reality moves on, and

3. Anthropology reveals how instinctive drives evolve.
   Love, hate, fear and altruism help in forming our resolve;
   to make a time where human conflicts in the world dissolve:
   reality moves on thereof.

4. Our ancestors' ancient myths and fears are mostly now extinct.
   Neuroscience has now shown how and why we behave and think.
   Imagination and creativity provide the link;
   reality moves on in synch.

5. Solving mysteries of DNA and human genome
   are feats that show the mind of science is not asleep at home.
   Ventures into unknown space by daring thoughts and deeds have shown:
   reality moves are not alone.

6. Human minds have brought great joy and helped our lives today;
   music, art and science written down by hand or other way;
   continue making progress toward utopia some day.
   Reality moves on this way.

Index

A
Agricultural Extension Service 42
American Friends Service Committee   157, 165
Anaconda Copper Company 45
anthropomorphism 143

B
Bacon, Sir Francis 140
bamboo 57, 59-61
    Fiber & papermaking characteristics 60
    research support 61, 63
        Monsanto 63-64
Balmer, Randall
    Thy Kingdom Come: How the Religious Right Distorts the Faith and Threatens America 123
Bank of North Dakota   140
Barton, Bruce
    and European fascism   132
    The Man Nobody Knows 130
    adviser to Coolidge, Hoover, and Willkie 131
Battelle Memorial Institute 45
Batten, Barton, Durstine & Osborne 130
Becker, Ernest
    The Birth and Death of Meaning 118
Beechcraft   38
Bellamy, Edward   19-20
    Looking Backward 19
Berea College 28-29
    Bible studies   29
    Berea Folk Dancers   29
Bergson, Henri   119
    Creative Evolution   120
Bernoulli's principle   36
Bible 131, 133, 140, 158
    gospels 29
    justification for war   133

Bible (*cont'd*)
    justification for slavery 135
    inerrancy 158, 160
    lessons 7, 8
    the Lord's Prayer (Matthew)   8, 145
    Martin Luther at Eisenach   94
    New Testament 130
    skepticism 48-49
    Twenty-third Psalm   144
    text, *Book of Common Prayer*   145
Big Bang, the 150-151
Binghamton, NY   9
"Biology of Ultimate Concern" 116-117
    and fundamentalism 133
Blackwell, Maud   5
Blue Angels   38
Bothwell, Cecil
    The Prince of War: Billy Graham's Crusade for a Wholly Christian Empire 135
Bryan, William Jennings 119
Burr, Amelia Josephine
    A Song of Living   76
Bush, George W.
    and David Kuo   132

C
Calvin, John   119
Cannabis (hemp)   57
Carroll, Jill in Iraq   103
Carter, Jimmy   122
    Carter Center   164
    and fundamentalism   131
    and Habitat for Humanity   164
Cherokee Removal Act 133
Citizens United 111
Clemson University   64-67
    Haun scale development   66
Clinton, Hillary 163

Clinton, Hillary (*cont'd*)
  on Planned Parenthood   163
Coca Cola   66
  MinuteMaid   67
Cold War
  Reinhardsbrunn Symposium   90-92
  Luther, Martin   94
    Wartburg Castle, Eisenach   94
  espionage 93-94
common ancestry   159
Common Cause   106
Commonwealth & Southern Corp.   20
  versus TVA   20
  and Wendell Willkie   20
Congregational church   4, 50
  Columbia, CT   7
  Le Raysville, PA   7
Constable, John   4
Conway, Ark. *see* War
Coolidge, Calvin
  and Bruce Barton   131
Copernicus, Nicholas   119, 140, 169
cortisone   55
  steroidal derivatives   55
Council for Secular Humanism   146
Coyne, A. J.
Why Evolution Is True   159
Crambe abyssinica   56
creative imagination *see* Humanism
Crotolaria   57-59
cultural evolution   131, 160-161, 169-170
Cumberland Homesteads 21-22, 24,
  26-27, 139

D

Darwin, Charles 119, 125, 140, 142-143,
  146, 159, 169-170
Dawkins, Richard
  The God Delusion   123
Democratic Party   40, 42-43, 105

Dennett, Daniel
  Breaking the Spell   123
  Darwin's Dangerous Idea   123
Depression   131, 139
Dewey, Thomas E.   43
Dickinson, Boonsri   151
digitalis   55
Dioscorea   55
Dobzhansky, Theodosius   116, 118, 120
Doughnut Corporation of America   52
Downey, Rep. Thomas   110
Draycot house *see* Smith, John
DuBois, James   107
DuPont Corporation   43
  employment   46-47, 51-52
  history   47
Durant, Will (and Ariel)   156
  The Story of Civilization   156
  The Story of Philosophy   116
  The Truth About the Truth   116

E

East Germany *see* Cold War
Edinburg, VA   3
Edison, Thomas Alva   155
Education
  Bible *see* Bible
  college   27
    Antioch   28
    Beloit   28
    Berea   27-29, 40-42
    Oberlin   28
  elementary   15, 17, 25-26
  G I Bill of Rights   40-42
  graduate school   45
  high school   27
  master's degree   45
  PhD   44-45, 167
  scientific method   15, 167
    of egg production   15

Education, scientific method (*cont'd*)
   versus religion   30
   Scott, Sir Walter   27
   Settlement Schools   26
   sex   25-26
   University of Chicago   41
   University of Maryland   42
Eisenhower, Dwight   43
Ethical Culture Society 54, 105, 158, 161
   Ethical Society of Asheville   105
evolution, Darwin's theory of   119
   features of   159
   versus Creationism   159

F

Fairchild, David   54
Faith *see* Religion
fallen evangelists   132
   see also Religion, unethical behavior
Falwell, Jerry   124
"the Family"   129-130, 132
   anti-Communism   132
   Billy Graham   132
   and European fascism   132
   and international dictators   132
   McCarthy, Sen. Joseph 132
   National Prayer Breakfast   132
Farming
   animal husbandry   3-5, 14, 23
   butchering a hog   22-23
   egg production   14-15
   Rhodes family   5
   harvests   4, 6
fascism 132
FDR *see* Roosevelt, Franklin D.
Federal Deposit Insurance Corp.   42
"the Fellowship"
   see "the Family"
Fennell, Sharon
   Memories of Ruth 76-78

Fisk University   13
   James Weldon Johnson   13
Ford, Gerald
   and Suharto in Indonesia 132
Fort Oglethorpe   4
Fowler, Sen. Wyche   110
foxglove   55
Free Inquiry   146
   see also Humanism
Freud, Sigmund   143
Fried, Richard   130
Fuller, Millard and Linda   164
fundmentalism *see* religion

G

Galileo Galilei   119
Gandhi, Mohandas   105
Ghadiri, Reza 152
GI Bill of Rights   40, 41, 42
Gilded Age   108
gradualism   159
Graham, Billy 132, 135
Grand Ole Opry   13
Grandma Smith *see* Smith, Leila
Great Depression *see* Depression
Great Society   108
Grumman F7F Tigercat   38
Guenther Brewing Company   52

H

Habitat for Humanity   163
Haggard, Ted   132
Harris, Sam   123
   The End of Faith   123
   Letter to a Christian Nation   123
Hartford Theological Seminary 4
Haun, Alan 48, 68, 72, 88, 140
Haun, Charles   4, 160
   Cumberland Homesteads 22
   Democratic policies   131

Haun, Charles (*cont'd*)
  and Lydia (Rhodes) 4-5
  and James Weldon Johnson 13
  and John Frederick Oberlin 17
  ministerial duties 4, 7-10, 18, 122, 131
  and race relations 13
  and TVA, Knoxville 16
  at Vanderbilt U. 4, 9-10, 12, 122
  violin 8, 13
  World War I 4, 34
Haun, David 52, 72, 88, 140
Haun, Elizabeth 4
Haun, Helen 88
  Parents Without Partners 88
  travel 88-89
Haun, Jeffrey 53, 68, 72, 88, 140
Haun, John 4
Haun, Lydia
  and Charles 4-5
  Lynchburg College 7
  piano 8
Haun, Margaret (Johnson) 88
  piano 13
Haun, Michael 53, 68, 72, 88, 140
  ski vacation 90, 95
Haun, Raymond 4
Haun, Ruth 29, 33, 41-43, 67-68, 71-73, 87, 97
  cancer 73, 140
  death 73, 75
    Memories from Sharon Fennell 76
    treatments 74
  family life 48, 70
  Grandma Smith 67-68, 71
  League of Women Voters, Clemson 67
  religious choices 48-49
  Unitarian Fellowship, Clemson 67
Haun scale 66, 73, 153
  and Quantitative Morphology 66-67
Haun, Steven 48, 72, 96-97, 99-100, 140
  Anne Squires Haun 97
  Warren Wilson College 88, 96
Haun, Virginia 4
hemp (*Cannabis*) 57-59
  seed supply 58
Henley, William Ernest 154-155
  "Invictus" 154
Herty Foundation 59
Hibiscus cannabinus (kenaf) 57
Higgins, Joseph 153
  Seabrook Frozen Seafood Company 56
  USDA New Crops Branch 57
Hitchens, Christopher 123
  God is Not Great 123
Hogness, T. R. 41
home construction (*see* house building)
Hoover, Herbert
  and Prohibition 26
  and Bruce Barton 131
horses
  in agriculture 5, 6
  Percheron 3
  Clydesdales 9
house building
  Beltsville, MD 53
  Clemson, SC 67-68
  masonry 97-100
  Newark, DE 48
  Swannanoa, NC 96-97, 100-101
  well drilling 68-70
Humanism 54, 103, 120, 146-147
  adherents 146-147
  "The Biology of Ultimate Concern" 116-117
  creative imagination 102, 143-145, 168-169
  cultural evolution 131, 169
  definition 149
    Paul Kurtz on 146-147
  Enlightenment thought 116

I

imagination   145
  human evolution of   143, 169
Indian snakeroot   55
Influenza epidemic of 1918   4
intelligent design   120
"Invictus," W. E. Henley   154

J

Jackson, Andrew
  and Native Americans   107, 133
  Cherokee Removal Act 133
  Trail of Tears   133
  Treaty of Echota   133
Jackson, "Stonewall"   133
Jefferson, Thomas   5
  Dumas Malone biography   5
  Monticello   5
Jesus   130-131
Johnson, James Weldon   13
  God's Trombones   13
Johnson, Lyndon   108, 136
  The "Great Society"   108
Jordan, Clarence   164
Jung, Carl   143

K

Karaball, Zachary   43
Katz, Steven: "How to Speak and Write Postmodern"   117
Kauffman, Dr. James M.
  and "Dr. Laura" letter   160-161
kenaf (*Hibiscus cannabinus*)   57-59
Kennecott Copper   45
Kennedy, John F.   136
Kepler, Johannes   119
King, Dr. Martin Luther, Jr.   105
Koresh, David   126
Kostmayer, Sen. Pete   110
Kowalski, Gary   104, 142

The Souls of Animals   104, 141
Knoxville, TN   16
Krieg, Margaret   55
Kuo, David   132
Kurtz, Paul
  "Secular Humanism Is..."   146

L

Le Raysville, PA   7
League of Women Voters, Clemson   67, 76
Lennon, John
  "Imagine"   114
Lilienthal, David   18-21
  and C&S   20
  versus A. E. Morgan   20-21
Lord's Prayer, The   8, 145
Lucas   101-102, 142
Luther, Martin   94-95
Luziane Coffee   52
Lynchburg College   7

M

marijuana   58
masonry   *see* house building
McCain-Feingold   111
McCarthy, Sen. Joseph   132
Mexican yam   55
"Monkey Trial"   119
Miller, Stanley   150-151
Minimum Wage Law   42
MinuteMaid   67
Mitchell, Sen. George   110
Mondragon Cooperative   139
money and politics *see* politics and money
Monsanto   63
Morgan, Arthur   18-20
  and C&S   20
  fired by Roosevelt   21
  versus Lilienthal   20-21
Morgan, Harcourt (H.A.)   18, 20

Murfreesboro, TN 11
Myth 117-119

N

Nashville 9-10, 12
  Parthenon 12
  Ryman Auditorium 12-13
National Prayer Breakfast *see* "the Family"
natural selection 159
Naval Reserve *see* War
New Deal 16, 42, 131, 139
Nixon, Richard 108
Norris, Sen. George W. 18

O

Oberlin, John Frederick 17

P

Paderewski, Ignacz 13
Panama Canal
  DuBois, James 107
  Nixon, Richard 108
  Roosevelt, Theodore 107
  United Fruit Company 108
  Wilson, Woodrow 108
Parents Without Partners 88
Park Chung Hee
  and "the Family" 132
Parthenon
  Athens 12
  Nashville 12
Penny, Rep. Tim 110
Pensacola, FL 38
Phelps Dodge Corporation 45
Phillips, Kevin 134, 136-137
  American Theocracy, the Peril and Politics of Radical Religion, Oil, and Borrowed Money in the 21st Century 134-135
Piper Club 36

Planned Parenthood 162-163
Poe, Edgar Allan 5
politics
  see also Democratic Party; Religion
  and money
    Citizens United 111
    "Clean Money" 111
    Downey, Rep. Thomas 110
    Fowler, Sen. Wyche 110
    Kostmayer, Sen. Pete 110
    McCain-Feingold 111
    Mitchell, Sen. Ted 110
    Penny, Rep. Tim 110
    public financing in NC 112, 157
Prohibition 26
  Berea College 28
  FDR 26
  Hoover, Herbert 26
  Women's Christian Temperance Union 26

R

Race
  Berea College 28
  Charles Haun interest 13
  Jackson, Andrew 107
  Nazi theories 103
  and political affiliation 135
  terminology 11
  and voting rights 106-107, 135
rapeseed 56
"Reality Moves On" 148, 191
Religion *see also* Humanism
  anti-democracy 134
  cathedrals and monuments 72, 90
    Lourdes 118
    Tintern Abbey 96
  Congregationalism 4, 50
  creationism 149
    versus evolution 158-159
  and family 48-49, 122

Religion (*cont'd*)
  fundamentalism (*also* fundamentalists)
    129, 131, 133-134, 160, 170
  heaven and hell   103
  Inquisition   89
  and myth   117, 119, 126
  and politics
    Common Cause   106
    ethical behaviors   106
      see also Politics and money
      Gandhi, Mohandas   105
      the golden rule   129
      Johnson, Lyndon
        The Great Society   108, 136
      King, Dr. Martin Luther, Jr.   105
      New Deal   108
    Roosevelt, Theodore trustbusting   108
    "the Family"   129-130
    unethical behaviors
      Bakker, Jim   132
      Citizens United   111
      ethanol subsidies   108
      Fowler, Sen. Wyche   110
      Gilded Age   108
      Hargis, Billy James   132
      Jackson, Andrew   108
      Kostmayer, Sen. Pete   110
      mountaintop removal   108
      Penny, Rep. Tim   110
      Roaring '20s   105
      Roosevelt, Theodore in Panama   108
      S&L bailout   109
      Swaggart, Jimmy   132
    theocracy   134
    voting rights   106-107
  and science   117-119, 122, 133, 169
    biblical inerrancy   158, 160
    Big Bang, the   149-150
    Calvin, John   119
    Copernicus, Nicholas   119, 169
    creation   149
    Dark Ages   136
    Darwin, Charles   119, 125
    Galileo Galilei   119
    intelligent design   120
    Kepler, Johannes   119
    origin of life   149-152
    soul   102-104, 141
      of animals   141-142
      of children   144
    spirituality   103-104
    Transcendentalism   50
      Thoreau, Henry David   143
      "philosophic naturalism"   143
    Unitarianism   *see* Unitarian Church
Republican Party   40, 42-43
reserpine   55, 65
Reserve Officers Training Corps   *see* War
Rhodes   4, 5
  Carl   5
  Elizabeth   5
  Guy   5
    and Hazel 5
  Lydia 5
  Ralph 5
  Rosa   5
    and Guy Hockman   5
Roaring '20s   108
Roosevelt, Franklin D.   16
  Cumberland Homesteads   21, 139
  New Deal   16, 21, 108, 139
  Prohibition   26
  TVA   16, 18-21, 139
Roosevelt, Eleanor   21
  Cumberland Homesteads   21
Roosevelt, Theodore
  and Panama Canal   107
  trustbuster   108
Rosetti, Christina, Remember 75
Rural Electrification Act   42

Ryman Auditorium   12
   and Grand Ole Opry   13

S

safflower   56
Sanger, Margaret   162, 163
Sartoris, Nelson   136
   The American Disenlightenment   137
   the Big Bang   150-151
Scarlett's Seed Company   52
Schram, Martin
   Speaking Freely   110
Scopes see "Monkey Trial"
Scott, Sir Walter
   Ivanhoe   27, 72
   Lake Country   72
   Quentin Durward   27, 72
   Rob Roy   27
Seabrook Frozen Seafood Company 56
   C. W. Thornthwaite   56-57
   Joseph Higgins   56
Sharlet, Jeff
   The Family   129, 131, 133-134
      and historical innacuracy   133
      and homeschooling   133-134
   see also "the Family"
Shenandoah Valley   3
Shubin, Neil   160
Silva, Gen. Costas
   and "the Family"   132
Sisk, Tim   88
slavery, religious justification for   135
Smith, Leila ("Grandma")   67-68, 71
Smith, John   71, 97
Smith, Maureen   61
snakeroot   55, 65
Social Security   42
socialism   140
Soil Conservation Act   42
Sousa, John Phillip   12
soybeans   56
speciation   159
Spencer, Herbert   20
Stevenson, Adlai   44
Stevenson, Robert Louis
   Treasure Island   96
stone work   *see* house building
Suharto, Gen.
   and "the Family"   132
"survival of the fittest"   159

T

Tennessee Valley Authority (*see also* TVA)
   New Deal   16
Tephrosia   57
theocracy   134
Thoreau, Henry David   143
Thornthwaite, C. W.   56-57
   Seabrook Frozen Seafood Company   56-57
Tillich, Paul   117
Tobin, James
   Great Projects   19
Trail of Tears   133
Trapping animals   23
Treaty of Echota   133
Truman, Harry S   42-43
   and Civil Rights   136
Turner, J. M. W.   4
TVA   16, 18-21, 139
   versus C&S Corp.   20

U

Unemployment Compensation Act   42
Unitarian Church 49-50, 104, 105, 122, 161
   Fellowship of Beltsville, MD   53
   Fellowship of Clemson, SC   67
   UU Service Committee   157
Unitarian-Universalists *see* Unitarian Church
United Fruit Company   108
University of Virginia, Charlottesville   4

Urey, Harold   150-151
(US Department of Agriculture)   53, 63, 65
  Crops Research Division 54
  New Crops Research Branch   54
    Joseph Higgins   56-57, 153
  Wine sale grants 108

V

Van Gogh, Vincent   6
  "La Moisson" (The Harvest)   6
Vanderbilt University   4, 9, 10
Voneff Candy Co. 52

W

Willkie, Wendell   20
  and Bruce Barton   131
  and Commonwealth & Southern Corp.   20
  and TVA   20, 21
Wilson, E. O.   117-118, 120, 122
Wiseman, Phil   5
Wiseman, Rob   5
War
  World War I   4, 34
  World War II   33
    Beechcraft   38
    Bernoulli's principle   36
    Conway, AR   36
    G.I. Bill of Rights   40, 41, 42
    Grumman F7F Tigercat   38
    Manhattan Project   41
    Memphis, TN   37
    Naval Reserve   34
    Pensacola U.S. Naval Air Station   38
    Piper Cub   36
    Quakers and pacifism   34
    ROTC   34
Workers Compensation   42

Y

YMCA   4, 34

www.ingramcontent.com/pod-product-compliance
Lightning Source LLC
Chambersburg PA
CBHW060516100426
42743CB00009B/1342